DUBLIN

TRADITIONS

DUBLIN
TRADITIONS

hamlyn

Publishing Director: Alison Goff
Executive Editor: Mike Evans
Editors: Humaira Husain, Michelle Pickering
Production Controller: Louise Hall
Picture Research: Charlotte Deane
Creative Director: Keith Martin
Executive Art Editor: Geoff Fennell
Design: Martin Topping

First published in 2000 by **Hamlyn** an imprint of Octopus Publishing
Group Limited, 2–4 Heron Quays, London E14 4JP

Copyright © Octopus Publishing Group Limited 2000

Distributed in the United States by
Sterling Publishing Co., Inc.
387 Park Avenue South, New York, NY 10016–8810

A catalogue record is available for this book from the British Library

ISBN 0600 60006 8

Produced by Toppan Printing Co. Ltd
Printed in China

THE IRISH TIMES

THE IRISH TIMES

DUBLIN, SATURDAY, JULY 18, 1998

News Features

Face to Face

Pl... surgery
...ves out a

Has Ameri...

Weekend

Plus: Cooking...

HOME NEWS 3

Anjelica
sets up her
stall in
...oore St

Irish Independent

CITY SPECIAL

Saturday, July 18, 1998

The Examiner

saturday

£30 worth of FREE

the IRISH NEWS

Where words matter

Saturday, July 18, 1998   Edition: 38,833   35p (R. & GB 50p)

TODAY

Parents left behind

'We must walk' Orange leaders insist

By Tom Collins

Trial for
Juddmonte
PAGE 9
Swan's race

RACING POST

Saturday, July 18, 1998

Incorporating **The Sporting Life**

FRIDAY

...ke off marvellous Curragh...

Stalls sh...

PASTERNAK F...
TO TODAY'S GOLDEN...

FOR THE TIMES
WE LIVE IN

CONTRIBUTORS

1 ANNA SELBY is a freelance journalist for a variety of newspapers and magazines, and author of 11 books. She has particular interest in architecture and antiques.

2 DEBRA SELLMAN has a background in arts administration at leading London galleries, including the Saatchi Gallery and the Institute of Contemporary Art.

3 PAUL ROLAND is a freelance journalist and writer, a regular contributor to publications in the UK, Europe, US and Japan.

4 NATHANIEL HARRIS is a full time professional writer whose published titles include *Heritage of Ireland* (Hamlyn) and *The Easter Rising*.

5 CLARE CONNERY is a well known, food author, journalist, broadcaster and chef/restauranteur, who runs a food consultancy business from her home in Ireland.

6 DAVID SANDISON has written extensively on popular culture, especially music. He has spent 20 years in the music business and is a regular visitor to Ireland.

7 DIANA CRAIG is a much published author who has written with a particular interest in travel and mythology. Her books include *Myths Retold* (Hamlyn).

8 PATRICK CARROLL is a sports writer who has written extensively on the subject. Having lived in Ireland for nine years, he has considerable knowledge of Irish sporting life.

CONTENTS

ARC

The Custom House on the banks of the River Liffey was built by James Gandon, one of Dublin's leading Georgian architects, between 1781 and 1791. Its 38m (125ft) copper dome dominates the skyscape and is complemented by the building's elegant columns and colonnades, all reflected in the water below.

HITECTURE
8–31

The glory days of Dublin's architecture are, without doubt, firmly rooted in the Georgian period. Eighteenth-century Dublin saw a lively celebration of the new trends in building, from the neo-classical restraint of its elegant squares and the grand houses of the aristocracy to some remarkable feats of urban engineering. Much of this can still be seen by the visitor to Dublin today and, though some fine buildings were lost to the crass redevelopments of the 1960s and 70s, contemporary Dubliners are justly proud of their historic buildings and are now restoring them assiduously.

DUBH LINN

DUBLIN'S LOST CULTURES

What remains of an earlier Dublin – a medieval, a Viking, a Celtic or even prehistoric settlement? In fact, Dublin is generally regarded as a comparatively recent town in European terms. It celebrated its millennium in 1988, a date reckoned somewhat flimsily on its founding by Viking invaders in the 10th century. Long before this, though, there were small settlements, their artefacts preserved miraculously in Ireland's peat bogs. Newgrange – a particularly fine example of a prehistoric tomb – stands about 48km (30 miles) from present-day Dublin, a testament to an ancient culture.

The Celts began to arrive in Ireland before the birth of Christ, and maintained a uniquely uninterrupted civilization for centuries. During the same period, the rest of the British Isles were subjected to repeated invasions from the Romans, Angles, Saxons and Jutes. None of them crossed the Irish Sea, which left Celtic culture unsullied by outside influence. It was not, however, in the Celtic nature to build with a view to any sort of permanence, so there are virtually no visible remains from the period, though there is one important memento. The name Dublin comes from the Celtic Dubh Linn, meaning Black Pool and referring to the settlement's safe harbour at the point where the River Poddle met the Liffey.

Christianity came to Ireland around the beginning of the 5th century, with the patron saint Patrick, who, also according to legend, rid the country of its snakes (there are still no snakes to be found in Ireland). The Vikings arrived at the end of the 8th century, took control of the small Celtic settlement and encircled it with a stone wall. Although much of the Viking settlement acted simply as a base for raids, the Vikings soon began to live and indeed die there – early graves were found in Kilmainham cemetery, the largest Norse graveyard outside Scandinavia. Sadly, nothing visible remains of the Norsemen in Dublin – a wooden quay and the foundations of the walls and streets of

TOP An excavation for Viking artefacts and footpaths taking place in Dublin in 1968.

ABOVE Detail of a delicately curved bronze bit, originally part of a chariot harness, that was found in a bog. It dates from the 1st century AD.

OPPOSITE The Bronze Age monument of Newgrange, a distinctive mound surrounded by vertical chalk sides, is a prehistoric tomb believed to have been used for ritualistic purposes by the ancient Druids.

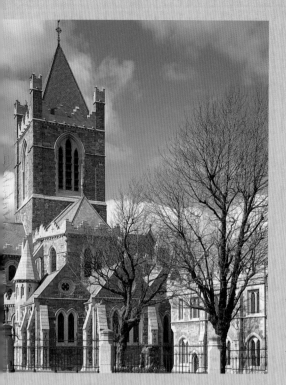

ABOVE Christ Church Cathedral, the first stone building in Dublin, was built by Richard Fitzgilbert de Clare, better known as 'Strongbow', whose tomb is believed to lie within.

BELOW Kilmainham cemetery is the largest Norse graveyard outside Scandinavia.

OPPOSITE The medieval cathedral of St Patrick's, which, according to legend, is built on the site where the saint baptised his converts to Christianity.

their settlement have disappeared. In the 1970s, the Civic Offices were built on the site, in spite of a public outcry.

SAINTS AND SOLDIERS

The first people to leave traces of their civilization behind were the Normans. They had already expanded from their lands in Normandy, in northern France, to conquer England in 1066. A century later, the Earl of Pembroke, Richard FitzGilbert de Clare – better known as 'Strongbow' – took Dublin. It was Strongbow who built the first stone building in Dublin – Christ Church Cathedral, for the Archbishop of Dublin, Laurence O'Toole. It replaced an earlier wooden building and, while it in turn has been transformed over the intervening centuries according to the tastes of the day, what is thought to be the tomb of Strongbow, bearing his effigy, can still be seen in the cathedral. Laurence O'Toole, incidentally, became the patron saint of Dublin, although he is buried in Normandy, where he died on a pilgrimage rather than in the cathedral.

The old Norman cathedral can still be glimpsed in places, such as the crypt with its stocky arches and the south transept, but it was largely rebuilt during its restoration in the 16th century. In the 19th century, it was restored once again with a few Victorian Gothic additions.

Dublin has a second medieval cathedral, St Patrick's, founded in 1191 on the site of an earlier wooden church. Legend has it that St Patrick himself baptised his converts at a well here. In fact, much of the cathedral was rebuilt in the 19th century as it had fallen into such a poor state of repair. Little of what can be seen today is actually part of the original building. St Patrick's most famous dean was Jonathan Swift, author of *Gulliver's Travels*. He was dean from 1713 to 1745 and is buried in

the cathedral. Within St Patrick's Close is Marsh's Library, already in use in Swift's day. Built in 1701, it has a collection of 25,000 books and manuscripts and unique caged-in alcoves, specially built to prevent any readers stealing the precious books.

The only other remaining medieval building in the city is Dublin Castle. It was built on the site of the original Viking stronghold in the early part of the 13th century. From that period, only the Record Tower and the Castle Yard, with its recently excavated segments of tower and walls, remain. The rest of the building does not look much like a castle at all and was repeatedly rebuilt over the centuries by the British administration as their headquarters. Nowadays, it is most often visited for its gloriously decorated Georgian state apartments with their grand staircase of Connemara marble.

FORTRESS DUBLIN

Dublin Castle's history is, of course, closely tied to the turbulent relationship between England and the Irish capital. For most of its recorded history, Dublin has been governed from London and, from the Normans onwards, it has been an invader's stronghold, with the rest of Ireland, literally, 'beyond the Pale' – the Pale being the wall that protected

DUBLIN CASTLE

ABOVE Trinity College is the most prestigious university in Ireland. Its alumni include such literary greats as Jonathan Swift, Oscar Wilde, Samuel Beckett and Bram Stoker.

OPPOSITE Dublin Castle's Record Tower, which, alongside Castle Yard, forms the extant remains of the site's original 13th-century building.

FOLLOWING PAGE Trinity College's Long Room, with its magnificent barrel-vaulted ceiling, holds over 200,000 books.

the English territories from the Irish beyond. It was only in 1922 that Dublin was finally restored to the rest of Ireland, as its capital and seat of government, and, in the intervening centuries, the influence of English style and taste had made its mark on the city's architecture.

Significantly, both St Patrick's and Christ Church Cathedrals are part of the Anglican Church of Ireland, and the Roman Catholic cathedral, St Mary's Pro-Cathedral, was built much later in 1829, coinciding with Catholic emancipation – the Catholic religion having been previously outlawed by the Protestant political and mercantile elite.

The most famous and grandest university in Ireland, Trinity College, founded by Queen Elizabeth I, was also exclusively for Protestants. Alumni include Oscar Wilde, Samuel Beckett, Jonathan Swift and Bram

Stoker, creator of *Dracula*. Catholics were
officially allowed to become students in 1873
but it is only in the past few decades that they
have joined in any significant number. Most
of the buildings date from the 18th century,
the elegant colonnaded façade typical of the
period. There are two libraries among
Trinity's seven that should not be missed.
The Old Library is home to *The Book of Kells*,
undoubtedly the greatest Celtic illuminated
gospel in existence. The other library that has
to be seen is the Long Room, with its shelves
of 200,000 books rising to the extraordinary
barrel-vaulted ceiling. The Long Room is
also home to 'Brian Ború's harp' – Brian
being the high king of Ireland in the 11th
century. This is the harp that appears on Irish
coins, but dates from around four centuries
after the death of Brian.

While the Catholic majority of the city
formed an underclass, from the end of the
17th century onwards the Protestants took
control of Dublin on every level. After the
significant defeat of the Catholic English king
James II by William of Orange (otherwise
known as Sweet William to the Protestants,

Stinking Billy to the Catholics) at the Battle of Boyne in 1691, the Anglo-Irish Protestants felt secure enough in their hold on the city to create from this besieged quarter of the empire a beautiful and elegant new Dublin, extending far beyond the old city walls. While the bitter political after-effects were to last for centuries, there can be no argument that, in this tenuous peace, an exquisite Georgian city was born.

GEORGIAN DUBLIN

From the earliest years of the 18th century, elegant terraces and squares sprang up to house the wealthy Anglo-Irish citizens of Dublin. While one of the great delights of Georgian architecture is that individual houses would often have unique touches of personality, they all conformed to a particular formula so there was an overall uniformity within the row. Georgian style was based on the designs of classical antiquity, as revived and interpreted by architects such as Palladio and Inigo Jones, who instigated a sense of classical proportion, columns and colonnades and a restraint enlivened by surface decoration in the form of ornate plasterwork and friezes and gracious stairways.

In essence, the Georgian house was divided hierarchically. The first floor, or *piano nobile*, was the focus and the centre of all entertaining. This floor would have the largest rooms with high ceilings and large windows, often opening onto decorative wrought-iron balconies. Internally the *piano*

BELOW Merrion Square exemplifies Dublin's Georgian architectural heritage. Former residents include Oscar Wilde and W B Yeats.

FITZWILLIAM SQ

nobile frequently had elaborate friezes, plasterwork on the ceilings and elegant fireplaces. The ground floor had smaller reception rooms, while the basement housed the kitchens. The second floor had the family's bedrooms and, above those, were the servants' rooms.

The window size reflected the underlying hierarchy – the first-floor windows were the largest, those on the top floor the smallest. Externally, the walls could be plain brick or stuccoed. The classical theme was reflected in ornate porticoes, columns, pilasters, fanlights, architraves and pediments – often the most exuberant elements in a restrained design. Besides the houses themselves, there were Georgian covers in the pavements of the streets, from which coal was poured into the coal holes below.

There are many squares and terraces in Dublin where you can see some fine examples of Georgian architecture. Merrion Square, with its pretty central garden, is one of the best known, especially as it has had more than its fair share of famous residents. Oscar Wilde was born at number one, the poet W B Yeats lived at different times at both numbers 52 and 82, while adjacent Upper Merrion Street was the birthplace of the Duke of Wellington. Another lovely square is Fitzwilliam Square and, in the adjoining Fitzwilliam Street Lower, there is a perfectly restored house, open to the public, at number 29. The house is presented very much as it would have been lived in towards the end of the Georgian period, and contains not only its original fittings but also furniture that would have typically been in the house at the time.

An even grander example of a restored Georgian building is Newman House on St Stephen's Green, actually two houses that were used as part of the first Roman Catholic university allowed in the city. The rector was Cardinal Newman – hence the name – and they are now open to the public and reveal the elegance of Georgian living. A particularly beautiful feature, and typical of its time, is the exquisite plasterwork of the ceilings.

St Stephen's Green has many other key Georgian buildings, such as the fine Royal College of Surgeons, but its most impressive must be Leinster House. It was originally built in 1745 as the home of the Duke of Leinster, but is now the Irish parliament and

OPPOSITE Fitzwilliam Square is a lovely enclave of Georgian terraces.

BELOW The Georgians delighted in ornate details, such as this footscraper, examples of which abound in Dublin's streets.

contains both the Dáil Éireann (parliament) and the beautiful stuccoed interior of the Seanad Éireann (senate).

Besides the terraces, squares and fine mansions, numerous public buildings were built in Georgian Dublin. One leading architect of the day was James Gandon, who built the Four Courts, the Custom House, the portico of the Old Parliament (now the Bank of Ireland) and the King's Inns. The Four Courts building stands on the banks of the River Liffey, its elegant columns reflected in the water, and, as its name suggests, it is a courthouse – though there are actually five rather than four courts. Built according to the grandest of Palladian principles, it has a central colonnaded upper level, topped by a copper dome. Gandon's Custom House took ten years to build and its 38m (125ft) copper dome towers above the surrounding buildings. It is a beautifully proportioned building with a portico of Doric columns and also stands on the banks of the Liffey.

ABOVE One of the statues adorning the façade of Dublin's Custom House.

BELOW The portico of the Bank of Ireland, formerly the Old Parliament.

BANK OF IRELAND

ABOVE The restored Georgian building Newman House was once part of Dublin's first Catholic university. The ornate plasterwork ceilings are typical of the period.

RIGHT The Four Courts building on the banks of the River Liffey. Its elegant columns and copper dome exemplify the grand Palladian principles favoured by the Georgians.

SHRINES AND PUNISHMENTS

It was not only gracious homes and civic institutions that appeared in Dublin in the 18th century. One of the landmarks of Dublin is the Guinness brewery, founded in 1759 and now housing a museum that is a virtual shrine to Ireland's national drink. Two-and-a-half million pints of the black stout with creamy head are still produced there every day – and visitors to the museum are given a glass to sample.

It has to be said that the pubs serving all that Guinness are almost a symbol of Dublin – so much so that Irish 'theme pubs' can now be found all over the world, in places as far from the Emerald Isle as Moscow and Abu Dhabi, though they cannot hope to capture the atmosphere of a real Dublin pub. James Joyce mentioned Davy Byrne's pub in *Ulysses* and it is still there today.

Traditionally, the Dublin pub was dark and crowded and filled with political discussion – and you can still find such places today. More often, though, changing trends have meant all manner of pub styles, from those offering traditional Irish music to vast drinking emporiums selling beers and spirits from all over the world. Interestingly, the demon drink has played a major part in Dublin's great religious buildings – a member of the Guinness family funded the restoration of St Patrick's Cathedral, while Henry Roe, a distiller, did the same for Christ Church.

There is a famous drinking house of quite another sort in Dublin – Bewley's café. This has now turned into a chain of coffee houses,

ABOVE The Guinness brewery's visitor centre is popular both for its exhibits detailing the history the famous drink and for the glass of the 'blackstuff' that visitors are given at the end of their tour.

LEFT Guinness's Hopstore brewery, home to Ireland's national drink.

OPPOSITE The Guinness brewery, founded in 1759, still produces two-and-a-half million pints of Guinness every day.

ABOVE A plaque outside Kilmainham Gaol commemorating the leaders of the Irish nationalist cause who were executed there after the Easter Uprising of 1916.

BELOW The interior of Kilmainham Gaol, which now houses an exhibition recounting the story of Irish nationalism.

with marble-topped tables, characteristically milky coffee and, in some cases, wooden pews and flamboyant stained-glass windows. Ernest Bewley was descended from a Quaker family who had moved to Ireland at the very beginning of the 18th century to escape religious persecution in England. His father, Joshua Bewley, had had a teashop in Sycamore Alley in the 1840s but Ernest decided coffee was the new trend. His cafés in Westmoreland Street and, later, Grafton Street were enormously popular and remain a much-loved institution in Dublin today.

Kilmainham Gaol, near the Guinness brewery, is a rather more chilling type of institution. This gloomy grey fortress has been compared to the Bastille in Paris, and it was built partly in response to the fact that French revolutionary ideas had spread to Ireland – and, indeed, led to the 1798 rising. Founded only a few years earlier, the gaol saw rebels and patriots incarcerated within its walls for 130 years. Now, however, it houses a moving – and often harrowing – retelling of the story of Irish nationalism.

Nearby is the Royal Hospital, Kilmainham, which is a hospital in the old sense of the word – a hospice for old soldiers. It was built in 1684 – making it older than Chelsea's Royal Hospital, home of the Chelsea Pensioners in London – and is now the Irish Museum of Modern Art.

ABOVE The Irish Museum of Modern Art, housed in the former Royal Hospital of Kilmainham.

TEMPLE

ABOVE The Ha'penny
Bridge, more properly
known as Liffey Bridge,
is a superb example of
Georgian cast-iron
industrial design.

OPPOSITE The Clarence
Hotel on the banks of the
Liffey is owned by the
rock band U2.

TEMPLE BAR

Temple Bar, the area along the south bank
of the Liffey between Trinity College and
Dublin Castle, has plenty of signs of its
18th-century origins, but it is also an
outstandingly successful escapee from 1970s
planning. Its death sentence was issued in
that benighted decade – it was to be
demolished to make room for a bus depot.
Rescued by the intervention of the then
Taoiseach (prime minister) Charles Haughey,
its low-rent buildings turned it into a haven
for artists and craftsmen in the 1980s, when
its atmosphere was poor but Bohemian. Since

then, it has gradually turned into Dublin's trendiest area, full of galleries, theatres, nightclubs, restaurants, cultural centres and street performers.

Temple Bar was very much a busy quayside area for centuries, and many of the original warehouses have now been developed into apartments, bars and restaurants as the commerce in the port has declined – a familiar pattern in many cities. Appropriately enough, it has Dublin's most famous bridge. Built in 1816 – for pedestrians only – it was first called Wellington Bridge after the duke, and is a typically elegant piece of Georgian cast-iron industrial design. Renamed Liffey Bridge after independence, it has always been affectionately referred to by Dubliners as Ha'penny Bridge – after the toll that used to be charged for crossing. Further westwards along the river bank is the Clarence Hotel (now owned by the rock band U2) and the Sunlight Chambers. This was built by the soap manufacturers, Lever Brothers, and has quite a unique terracotta frieze celebrating the wonders of soap.

There are two main squares – Temple Bar Square and Meeting House Square (named after its Quaker meeting house) – and lots of cobbled streets, just bursting with trendiness. There is a feeling among some Dubliners that

BAR

THE CLARENCE HOTEL

LEFT Crown Alley in the trendy, cobble-stoned Temple Bar district.

commercialism has started to take over and spoil the original bohemian, arty atmosphere as the streets have been pedestrianized and the new shops and restaurants have poured in. Having said that, if you are looking for the buzz of new Dublin, Temple Bar is most definitely the place to go.

However, Temple Bar as an area for setting cultural trends is nothing new. In fact, in the 18th century it was already a cultural centre. Fishamble Street (named after the 'shambles' or fish market) saw the first-ever performance of Handel's *Messiah* in 1742. The Charitable Music Society's hall where the premiere took place is, sadly, no longer there. However, the revival and restoration of Temple Bar into the city's liveliest and most vibrant area is a strong indication of how Dubliners are now taking the best of their architectural past with them into the future.

OPPOSITE St Stephen's Green shopping centre, a steel-and-glass splendour.

BELOW Meeting House Square is one of two main squares in the Temple Bar district. It is an ideal place to discover the delights of modern-day Dublin's architectural and sculptural inventiveness.

Interior of the National Gallery of Ireland in Merrion Square West. Opened in 1864, the gallery has a 2,000-strong collection representing every major school of European painting, and is a must-see attraction for all art-loving visitors to the city of Dublin.

Text: Debra Sellman

Dublin is celebrated as much for its dancers and musicians as it is for its writers and playwrights. The impact of artists on the city, however, has been more modest but no less important. James Malton's 18th-century aquatints of Dublin are familiar to many, but it is the recent economic boom that has done much to draw in new audiences for art and to introduce collectors to the auction rooms.

The 1998 annual report for the James Adam Salerooms lists record prices: Jack Butler Yeats' *Man versus Horse* sold for a staggering 300,000 Irish pounds and a new Irish record was set for *Dorothy and Irene Falkiner* by Walter Frederick Osborne, which halted bids at 355,000 Irish pounds. The upswing in art investment is partly rooted in the Irish government's favourable attitude towards collecting – the introduction of a 20 per cent reduction in the rate of capital gains tax has been a great incentive for many collectors to sell – and a developing sense of Irish-American nostalgia.

International interest in all things Irish has led to celebrated art shows both at home and abroad. 'Beyond the Pale: Art and Artists at the Edge of Consensus' in 1995 – the Pale refers to the palisade or fortified rampart built around Dublin in the 15th century by British colonists to keep out the native Irish – drew a record 230,000 people to the Irish Museum of Modern Art; and Imaginaire Irlandais, an Irish arts and culture festival held in and around Paris, was credited with introducing many Irish artists to the international scene.

THE CELTS

The 8th and 9th centuries mark the apogee of the Celtic period, whose masterpieces, such as the Ardagh Chalice and the Tara Brooch, are characterized by carved stone crosses, enamel and metalwork filigreed in gold and studded with jewels. *The Book of Kells*, a magnificent illuminated copy of the four gospels that dates from AD 800, is on permanent display at the Trinity College Library, and other Celtic antiquities can be found at the National Museum of Ireland and the Heraldic Museum.

These artistic outpourings were halted by successive invasions of the Vikings, Normans and English. The English colonial forces eventually dominated Ireland in 1537, land was appropriated and punitive laws against the Catholics were introduced. Subsequent uprisings and defeats followed, such as those put down by Cromwell, from 1641 to 1653, and by William of Orange, from 1689 to 1691. With colonization came the inevitable suppression of Irish culture and language. The great potato famine of 1845–1849 weakened the country and began an Irish Diaspora that has continued until recent years.

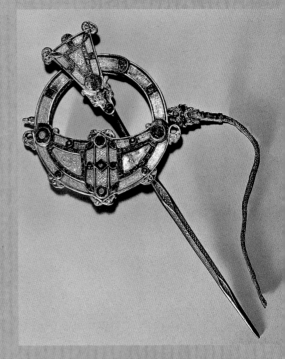

ABOVE The Tara Brooch, dating from the 8th century AD, is a masterpiece of gold filigreework, encrusted with semiprecious stones.

OPPOSITE *Dorothy and Irene Falkiner*, painted by Walter Frederick Osborne, set a new Irish record when it sold for 355,000 Irish pounds in 1998.

BELOW The beautiful bronze-and-gold Ardagh Chalice, found in a field near Ardagh, Limerick.

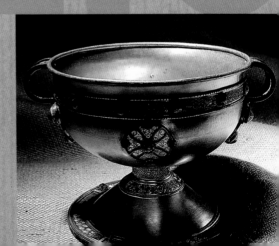

BARRET

ABOVE *View of Powerscourt, County Wicklow*, by George Barret c1760–62.

A CHANGING HISTORY UNDER COLONIALISM

The changing face of Irish art has by and large followed two main directions during the country's period as a colony: 'internationalism' and 'nativism'.

The international character of Irish work resulted from artists imitating styles that were current in London until the mid-1850s, then the Continent until the mid-20th century, and finally the United States during the 1970s. Indeed, many Irish painters emigrated to England in the 17th and 18th centuries. George Barret, for example, moved to London after training at the Dublin Society Schools and became a founder member of the Royal Academy. At the time, Ireland had little to offer painters in the way of education and artists looked for it abroad. In 1720, only the art academies of Paris, Rome, Florence and Bologna were comparable in teaching style to those of today. By 1790, however, there were over a hundred and the Dublin Society Schools formed part of that growth in art education.

The pull from abroad continued nonetheless and led many to Rome and Greece, countries that were especially popular with Irish artists in the late 18th century. Paintings by portraitists such as Hugh Douglas Hamilton were rich with depictions of the gardens of the Villa Borghese in Rome.

By the end of the 19th century, many Irish artists were living in Paris, and their work reflected a fascination with the techniques of impressionism and post-impressionism. Nathaniel Hone was the first to live there, then Sarah Purser, John Lavery, Roderic O'Connor and later William Leech. Interest in an Irish school of art also emerged concomitant with, but not dependent on, the Literary Revival. Eventually, the Society of Dublin Painters was established by Jack Yeats, Paul Henry and Mary Swanzy in 1920.

Nativism, the second direction, emerged around the time of the partition of Ireland. Eamon de Valera dominated Irish politics from 1926 to 1959 and official state art was used for political ends. By mythologizing peasant life and the landscape of the western, rural part of Ireland, the Celtic Revival managed both to play to British stereotypes and to celebrate an economic and cultural independence. As a result of this, figurative painting was never denigrated in Ireland as it was elsewhere and later, in the 1970s, painters such as Patrick Graham and Brian Maguire continued to use human imagery in their work.

While artists have consistently left Dublin, many have been attracted to the city. In the 1940s, a loose arrangement of foreign artists congregated under the name of the White Stag Group. Joseph Beuys also felt a strong connection to the city. Captivated by the bogs, botany and geology of Ireland, his 'Irish Energy' sculptures consisted of a pound of butter cemented between turf briquettes. During his visit to Dublin in 1974, he elaborated his ideas for a Free International University for Creativity, believing that as Ireland was the 'brain of Europe', Dublin would be the ideal location for such a centre. The university as an institution never materialized, but the ideas were discussed in one-hundred day conferences at the 1977 and 1982 Documenta in Kassel.

ABOVE The Irish painter John 'Jack' Butler Yeats, co-founder of the Dublin Painters Society in 1920.

FOLLOWING PAGE Detail of *Bogland Roskeeragh* by Seán McSweeney, from the cover of the catalogue accompanying the 1998 exhibition of his works, entitled 'Bogland & Shoreline Sligo', that took place at the Taylor Galleries in Dublin.

Seán

McSweeney

AROUND TOWN: COMMERCIAL GALLERIES, CONTEMPORARY SPACES AND STUDIOS

Young artists gravitate to the city to find commercial outlets, and the commercial gallery scene in Dublin centres on St Stephen's Green, south of the Liffey in the heart of the city.

Equipped with an *In Dublin* magazine, a *Gallery Guide* listings and a copy of *CIRCA*, Ireland's visual arts magazine, a walk around will reveal much of interest. Any visitor will discover that many of the galleries specialize in Irish artists. 'Most of the art-buying public in Dublin is interested Irish art,' believes David Britton of the Frederick Gallery, 'which is one of the reasons we decided to specialize in Irish art from 1880 to 1980.' The couturier-turned-gallerist Ib Jorgensen, who moved to Ireland in 1949, also focuses his collection on 18th-, 19th- and 20th-century paintings, drawings and watercolours by Irish and European artists.

The Taylor Galleries in Kildare Street are a good measure for contemporary work that continues the tradition of Irish landscape painting. Seán McSweeney's abstractions are self-taught: bog pools, shorelines and wetlands form his staple subject matter. His chewy paint surfaces fill the old Georgian house, formerly owned by the interior designer Charles Pilkington, with impact. This style, which has prevailed in Ireland since the late 1950s, has been challenged for some time.

Eilís O'Connell, for example, who shows at the Green on Red Gallery, attempts to convey a tension between natural and synthetic materials through abstract forms.

ABOVE Mural in the Setanta Centre – named after an Irish mythological figure – in Setanta Place off Nassau Street.

RIGHT 'Tower of Light' by Eilís O'Connell, a stainless-steel, resin and fibreoptic installation at the Green on Red Gallery, 1993–98.

She employs parrot feathers, cast resin, latex, lacquer and stainless-steel cable in her sculptures, and uses the rich archaeological remains of Ireland's prehistoric past as a fertile source of inspiration. Similar artists of international acclaim can be found in the Kerlin Gallery, situated off the main Grafton Street thoroughfare.

Other artists have less time for conceptualism and abstraction. The contemporary portraitists Blaise Smith and Oisin Roche both exhibit at the New Molesworth Gallery. Smith's subjects are Irish workers and Roche's portraits are in the style of Reynolds and Gainsborough. According to director Teresa Crowley, both artists 'look to the Irish portrait tradition of the style of Jack Yeats, Sean Keating and Sir William Orpen who, through their work, attempted to record an Irish character and humour that is peculiar to themselves.'

This sense of 'Irishness' is what draws many Americans to Dublin. Patrick Murphy, director of the Royal Hibernian Academy Galleries and former director of the Institute of Contemporary Art in Philadelphia, believes that Irish coverage in the United States still tends to be 'confined to the lyrical literary tradition' and he has criticized the fledgling Irish film industry for trading on the 'dual clichés of rural romanticism and urban violence'.

Many of these views are changing and, accordingly, artists have become receptive to public opinion. Crowley has noticed that 'younger artists today are much more commercially minded than ever before: if the work isn't selling, they believe that the public is trying to tell them something'. Access to studio spaces, many of which can be found in the north of Dublin, has also improved: an old clothing factory has been converted into the Palace Studios; North Side often has open days for the public; and The Fire Station maintains close links with the local community.

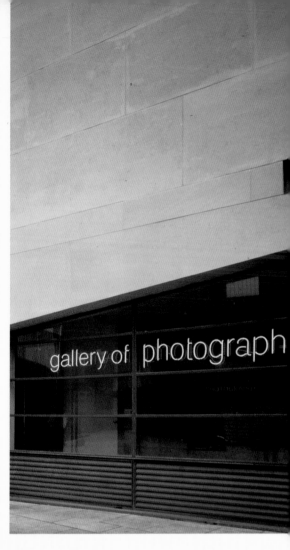

ABOVE The exterior of Dublin's Gallery of Photography, a popular attraction for tourists and locals alike.

TEMPLE BAR

Temple Bar Gallery and Studios is the largest studio and gallery complex in Ireland, situated along the Liffey quays, the visible face of arts in Dublin. Up to the 18th century, Temple Bar was a maze of small lanes and alleys. Today, the cobbled streets have been pedestrianized and the area stretches to the Ha'penny Bridge, which Dubliners would use – once they had paid the halfpenny toll – to avoid the murky ferry ride across the Liffey. With the demise of the traditional industries, the area fell into disrepair and stagnation until the European Regional Development Fund and the Ministry of Environment injected funds for regeneration.

Now, there are a number of interesting buildings and creative spaces among the brightly painted restaurants and knick-knack shops. The Original Print Gallery, for example, is a commercial gallery that exhibits work by Irish and international printmakers and co-exists with the Black Church Print Studio. The Gallery of Photography has a well-lit series of exhibition rooms in which it hosts an eclectic mix of touring shows: those

BELOW, LEFT & RIGHT
Interior of the Gallery of Photography. The minimalist setting provides the perfect backdrop for the photographic displays.

by local artists – most recently Irish-born Tom Wood's candid shots of the Merseyside environs – art school shows, and then those guaranteed to pull in the crowds such as Magnum photographer Elliott Erwitt's affectionate take on the canine world.

Arthouse, an impressive architectural design of glass, stone and steel, is aimed at pulling in the crowds from the 'New Media' generation. Born out of the cultural development programme and situated opposite the Music Centre, Arthouse offers training in multimedia courses and access to Artifact, a visual database of over 800 artists and their work. There is a definite buzz in the cyber café on the first floor, which offers internet access to its users, though one detects a hollowness to the chatter and a sense that the inhabitants would rather be talking to their computer screens than to one another.

OPPOSITE Performance artist Sandra Johnston uses repetitive movements to express personal sentiments that invite viewers to rethink the way in which they interact with their environment.

BELOW The glass, stone and steel creation Arthouse is a multimedia centre for the arts offering training courses and access to a visual database of artists.

SANDRA JOHNSTON

PERFORMANCE WORK AND WOMEN ARTISTS

One of the recent artists-in-residence at Arthouse is Sandra Johnston. Originally from Northern Ireland, Johnston arrived in Dublin in 1997 and found it so conducive to her working practice that she decided to stay there. At Arthouse, where she is conscious that artists often design their work to fit the workspace, her performances have attempted to 'make the building bend' to her work. Sophisticated studio machinery – digital multi-track recording and lighting systems, and video equipment – is used as a backdrop against which she struggles through repetitive movements of balancing, lifting objects and slow turns, to express personal sentiments that have wider implications, inviting onlookers to think again about their environment.

This endurance performance work has had as its progenitors Irish-born James Coleman, Scottish painter Alistair Maclennan and the English sculptor Nigel Rolfe. Their work was groundbreaking in the 1970s and continues to inspire a new generation of performance work. Through the use of body art,

storytelling with links to the oral tradition and rituals using totemic objects, these artists and collaborators found a response to the political and social turmoil in Northern Ireland, to the crisis of identity of the hero and ultimately to a wounded society that needed to heal.

Another of Johnston's performances was organized by Project Arts as part of their Offsite programme, which stages theatre performances and visual art projects around the city. In 1998, in a bedroom suite at the Ormand Quay Hotel, Johnston inhabited the space left by the previous guests. Fascinated by the 'the rapid cycles of usage and cleansing by day and by night' at the hotel, she observed the activity of persistent renewal as people pass through, 'their presence expressed in momentary traces, the slightest of touches'.

Project Arts was established by a group of practising artists in 1966, on the 50th anniversary of the Easter Rising of 1916. Its aims were to create a space for contemporary subversive art practice. At the time, the Catholic community in Dublin was highly

25 June – 31 July 1999 **JAKI IRVINE**

The Hottest Sun, The Darkest Hour
A Romance

influential in the state's activities and, though no exhibitions were actually banned, some experimental proposals were threatened with closure. In 1967, the Sheredon brothers' theatre-based work became a part of the group and a policy was introduced to use the building as a place for young bands.

Today, Project Arts is awaiting a new publicly funded building in the heart of Temple Bar, which Valerie Connor, the visual arts officer, hopes will 'continue the ethos – the identity – of the former building. To keep in line with history'. With this in mind, artist Jaki Irvine has been invited to curate the opening show in March 2000. Somewhere Near Vada will include 'time-based' video and film pieces by both famous and unknown artists. Her choice is driven by a desire to move away from shows that look towards MTV and the cinema as a critical and historical context for the work and a wish to bring work with 'all its inspirational potential' to a new Irish art audience.

Like many Irish artists, Irvine still maintains her connections with the city. 'Dublin', she considers, 'is not somewhere I think of in terms of having left behind, but rather somewhere I work both in and out of.' Her artistic contributions are diverse as a video artist, critic, writer and curator. Irvine's video, *The Hottest Sun, the Darkest Hour*, is a series of 16mm films projected simultaneously. Though they contain no obvious narrative, a sense of time and place and a way of being is slowly built up through the films. This progression is enhanced by questions about language, identity, intimacy, fantasy and memory. Her work was shown at the Douglas Hyde Gallery in July 1999, a gallery situated on the Trinity College campus, which is critically acclaimed for its solo shows of artists with international appeal.

Like Irvine in 1996, Anne Talentire represented Ireland at the Venice Biennale of 1999. Her work also has a subtlety that demands that the viewer absorb and reflect on the work over time. Unlike Irivine, however, Talentire's work is charged with a much greater political content. Her installation 'Bound words – stolen honey' from 1988 exhibits transcripts of the Brehnon beehive law that, to the horror of colonists of the 17th century, decreed that where the bees danced the honey was shared – across all boundaries of ownership.

Talentire is one of many women artists whose work concerns the role of women in Ireland. The unequal status of women in the eyes of the church, state, marriage and the workplace has meant that the practice of Pauline Cummins, Alice Maher, Kathy Prendergast, Alanna O'Kelly and Dorothy Cross has had an enormous impact. Often these artists employ unusual materials to make their point. Cross, for example, has used cowhides with teats to cover objects that are traditionally associated with feminine and masculine roles: an ironing board, a dressmaker's dummy, a saddle-horse. Happily, the roles of women in Ireland have begun to change: Mary Robinson was elected president in 1990; the abortion laws have been liberalized and there is now a growing female representation in the Dáil.

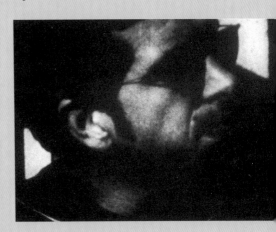

ABOVE Film still from *Marco, One Afternoon, 1998–99,* one of the films shown as part Jaki Irvine's *The Hottest Sun, The Darkest Hour* exhibition.

OPPOSITE Frontispiece of brochure promoting *The Hottest Sun, The Darkest Hour* by Jaki Irvine, shown at the Douglas Hyde Gallery in July 1999.

MUSEUMS

A taxi may not be the cheapest way to reach the Irish Museum of Modern Art (IMMA), which is some distance from the city centre but is well worth the outlay. Built to house retired soldiers at a time when Dublin remained architecturally a medieval city, Ireland's first 17th-century neo-classical building was inspired by Les Invalides in Paris. Later, it was used by the British as an army barracks. The museum was converted in 1991 to house an 800-strong collection and temporary shows, and was described by its director, Declan McGonagle, as an 'institutionalized alternative space', a 'function as well as a building'. To this end, McGonagle has injected life into the building through his Artists Work Programme, a series of ongoing residencies for local and international artists that have inspired panel discussions, workshops and a growing interaction with the public.

IMMA is home to the annual Glen Dimplex Artists Award – Catherine Yass won first prize in 1999 for her cibachrome

PREVIOUS PAGE Entrance hall of the Irish Museum of Modern Art. This 17th-century neo-classical building, originally used as a home for retired soldiers, now houses 800 permanent works as well as temporary exhibitions.

OPPOSITE One of the installations shown as part of the Irish Museum of Modern Art's *From Beyond the Pale* exhibition, by Mimmo Paladino, 1994.

BELOW The National Gallery of Ireland in Merrion Square West.

lightboxes of lonely hospital hallways and empty urinals – and has an established position alongside the Turner Prize in London and the recent Hugo Boss Prize in New York. Kathy Prendergast, another leading Irish artist of the younger generation, will be exhibiting *The City Drawings* at the museum over the new millennium. An ongoing project that began in 1992, it comprises hundreds of drawings of cities around the world and has been bought by the museum in its entirety.

Still on the south side, Merrion Square West is home to the National Gallery of Ireland, which opened in 1864 and sits next to the Natural History Museum. Among its

NATIONAL GALLERY

LEFT Interior of the
National Gallery of Ireland,
with its beautiful
chandeliered walkway and
sweeping staircases.

BELOW The Hugh Lane
Municipal Gallery of
Modern Art, Parnell
Square, Dublin.

2,000 piece collection, which represents every major school of European painting, is the Italian sculptor Antonio Canova's marble statue of Cupid, *Amorino*. In March 1999, the then Taoiseach, Mr Bertie Ahern, opened a museum in the gallery that is dedicated to Jack B Yeats, brother of poet William Butler Yeats.

A number of bequests have been made to the Irish state. The Chester Beatty Library and Gallery of Oriental Art has an impressive collection of rare books, miniature paintings and precious objects. They were donated by Sir Alfred Chester Beatty, an American mining millionaire and his collection of rhinoceros horn carvings are exquisite and well worth the visit. On the north side, the Hugh Lane Municipal Gallery of Modern Art was formerly a townhouse owned by Lord Charlemont and was opened in 1930 to display the collection of art collector Sir Hugh Lane.

Near the Hugh Lane Gallery, the James Joyce Centre promotes the writer's work and takes groups on tours to discover his north inner city. The museum that contains his letters, photographs and rare editions of *Ulysses* is situated in one of the Martello towers 14.5km (9 miles) south of Dublin. The Dublin Writers Museum, which boasts a ceiling by Michael Stapleton, is in the same northern district of Dublin as the Joyce Centre and features Samuel Beckett, W B Yeats, Oscar Wilde and George Bernard Shaw among others; the Irish Writers Centre next door often hosts a variety of readings of these great writers.

ABOVE Anna Livia's millennium fountain, depicting the goddess of the River Liffey, is more popularly referred to by Dubliners as 'The Floozie in the Jacuzzi'.

PUBLIC ART

A short stroll from this writers' corner is the Garden of Remembrance, a public park dedicated to the memory of all those who died for Irish freedom. In the centre is a sculpture by Oisin Kelley based on the myth of the Children of Lir who were changed into swans.

Public sculpture is common both north and south of the river. There is the bronze of James Joyce in North Earl Street and one of the mythical Molly Malone in Grafton Street. The aquatic sculpture of Anna Livia, the goddess of the River Liffey, features in Joyce's *Finnegan's Wake* and is commonly known as 'The Floozie in the Jacuzzi'.

The limestone relief that marks the entrance to the Department of Industry and Commerce in Kildare Street is an example of the unexpected decorative pleasures that it is worth stumbling across.

This image depicts Lugh, the god of light from Irish mythology, releasing a flight of aeroplanes, and was completed in 1942 by Gabriel Hayes. That Hayes was a woman created a stir for the press of the time. One journalist wrote that the work 'is characterized by the formal, unemotional, I might almost say unfeminine quality of stylized design' and another stated that 'I thought it amazing how so graceful and thin a hand could wield a five pound wooden mallet as if it were a pencil'.

Francis Street is worth a visit for anyone who is searching for a lasting souvenir of the city in the form of a sculpture or an antique. The centre of the antiques trade in Dublin, it features small shops and arcades that house fine examples of early Irish and English furniture. However, what better way to end the museum tour than with a visit to a museum that fondly touches the hearts and souls of most Dubliners: the Guinness brewery, founded in 1759, has its own visitor's centre and museum, the Guinness Hop Store. You will be sure to sample this piece of Irish history in the pub afterwards …

DRAMA & LITERATU
56—79

Brendan Behan (left) in 1952. Behan was a boist
Dublin intellectual who became legendary as a po
novelist, dramatist and ballad singer. He once bo
of being thrown out of every pub in the capital.

RE

J ames Joyce once ruefully remarked that he had not been just to the beauty of Dublin, but for Joyce and generations of great Irish writers from Jonathan Swift to Seamus Heaney, the beauty of the capital was to be found in the poetry of colloquial conversations, the drama of its larger-than-life characters and in the clamour of the overcrowded bars, decaying tenements and melancholic grandeur of the Georgian façades that served as the backdrop to their lives.

The tradition of Irish literature stretches back to the Gaelic civilization whose oral traditions included the Ulster and Fenian sagas that were preserved in manuscript form by monks and poets. However, after the exile of the last of the Irish lords in 1607, English became the language of government as well as trade and commerce. The majority of Irish writers and dramatists from the 17th century onwards adopted English as their first language, and many felt forced to settle in London in search of recognition and a reasonable livelihood.

18TH-CENTURY FICTION

The first great Irish writer in English was the satirist Jonathan Swift (1667–1745), whose parents were both English. His mother had been widowed shortly before the birth and returned to England soon after, leaving her son in the care of a wealthy uncle who enrolled the boy at Kilkenny College and then Trinity College, Dublin. He took holy orders in 1694 and, in 1713, became dean of St Patrick's Cathedral in Dublin (where a brass plaque marks his grave), but he refused to tone down his tirades against what he saw as the English colonization of Ireland and the collaboration of the Irish aristocracy. In 1720, Swift urged his fellow countrymen to 'Burn everything that comes from England except the coal', but he was rarely so direct. He preferred the double-edged sword of satire, which he wielded to considerable effect in *A Tale of a Tub* (1704), in which he lampooned the irrationality of religion, and in the allegorical *Gulliver's Travels* (1726), which has since become a children's classic. Jonathan Swift died a year after its publication. In his will he left money to found a hospital for the mentally ill, St Patrick's Hospital, and a verse to explain why he had done so.

> He gave the little wealth he had
> To build a house for fools and mad:
> And showed by one satiric touch
> No nation wanted it so much.

The novelist Lawrence Sterne (1713–68), author of the whimsical *The Life and Opinions of Tristram Shandy, Gentleman*, is commonly included in lists of Irish writers', but his link with Ireland is a tenuous one. He was born in Clonmel and lived as a child in Dublin, where his soldier father had been stationed, but he spent the rest of his life in

OPPOSITE Illustration of a scene from Jonathan Swift's *Gulliver's Travels*, which remains one of the most well-known and well-loved children's novels.

ABOVE Contemporary portrait of Jonathan Swift by Charles Jervas.

GOLDSMITH

England and did not allude to Ireland in his writing. However, the techniques and eccentric devices that he demonstrated in *Tristram Shandy* were to influence the 'stream of consciousness' style fashionable in the 20th century and exemplified by James Joyce.

18TH-CENTURY DRAMA

Irony, high spirits and a rapier repartee were the key themes of restoration comedy, as exemplified by George Farquhar (1678–1707), whose most successful plays, *The Recruiting Officer* and *The Beaux Stratagem*, are still popular today. Farquhar was born in Londonderry and had spent just two years at Trinity College before he left to join the cast of the nearby Smock Alley theatre company. However, neither academia nor acting proved his forte, and he abandoned the stage to be a playwright after accidentally wounding a fellow actor with a sword.

Novelist, dramatist and poet Oliver Goldsmith (1728–74) had an equally undistinguished tenure at Trinity, but he stayed the course and, after graduating, drifted aimlessly through Europe until settling for a career in journalism in London, where he befriended Dr Johnson, the dominant figure in London literary society. It was Johnson who sold the manuscript of Goldsmith's first novel, *The Vicar of Wakefield*, to get Goldsmith out of debt, thereby launching his friend on a literary career whose highlights included the poem *The Deserted Village* and the farce *She Stoops to Conquer*. Despite his success, however, Goldsmith died as he had lived, in debt.

Goldsmith's style of comedy was continued by the Dublin-born dramatist Richard Brinsley Sheridan (1751–1816), whose father was actor-manager of the Theatre Royal in Smock Alley. Sheridan followed his family to England at the age of eight and never returned to Ireland. His first success, *The Rivals*, was staged at Covent Garden while its author was only 24, after which he succeeded David Garrick as manager and owner of the Theatre Royal in Drury Lane. Further success followed with the robust comedy of errors *School for Scandal*, after which his energies were diverted into politics. He was elected member of parliament for Stafford in 1780, and established a reputation as a formidable orator, once making a speech lasting more than five-and-a-half hours. However, he lost much of his personal wealth when the Theatre Royal burnt down in 1809, after which he lost his seat, fell into debt and took to drink. He died in London and was buried in Poets' Corner at Westminster Abbey.

ABOVE Cyril Maude and Winifred Emery in a performance of *School for Scandal* by Richard Brinsley Sheridan.

BELOW Blue plaque marking Sheridan's home in Dublin's Merrion Square.

ABOVE Contemporary
portrait of Maria Edgeworth
by Joseph Slater. Although
Englishborn, Edgeworth
grew up in Ireland, and her
novels accurately depict
Irish rural life in the 18th
and 19th centuries.

19TH-CENTURY FICTION

Maria Edgeworth (1767–1849) was English by birth but she was brought up in Ireland on her father's extensive Longford estate. Her observant eye for detail and narrative skill captured the flavour and minutiae of Irish rural life, its dialect and customs in a series of novels, of which *Castle Rackrent* is the most memorable. This story of a family of profligate, indolent landlords was to prove a seminal influence on the early work of Jane Austen, Sir Walter Scott and a generation of French and Russian novelists.

Other popular Irish novelists of the period were Lady Morgan (1776–1859), author of *The Wild Irish Girl*, whose florid style has dated rather badly, but whose portraits of Irish life were influential in their day, as were the rural tales of John (1798–1842) and Michael Banim (1796–1874), Gerald Griffin (1803–40), William Carleton (1794–1869) and Charles Lever (1806–72). Irish verse, too, was enjoying a renaissance at this time under the pens of James Clarence Mangan (1803–49), Jeremiah Joseph Callanan (1795–1829) and Sir Samuel Ferguson (1810–86), whose plangent poetry evoked the ghosts of Ireland's pagan past.

However, not all of the Emerald Isle's writers drew inspiration from their history or surroundings. The characters created by Dublin-born Charles Robert Maturin (1782–1824), an eccentric clergyman with a passion for Gothic melodrama, inhabited an entirely different landscape. Maturin's best-known work, *Melmoth the Wanderer*, the tale of an immortal being, was to be cited as an influence by both Balzac and Baudelaire and is likely to have been a source of inspiration for Bram Stoker's *Dracula*. Maturin was curate of St Peters in Dublin from 1805 until his death. Bram Stoker

ABOVE Engraving of clergyman and novelist Charles Robert Maturin, 1819, whose passion for melodrama can be experienced in the splendid Gothic horror novel *Melmoth the Wanderer*.

RIGHT Drawing of Irish novelist Lady Morgan, c1830, whose florid writing style now seems rather dated but was popular during her lifetime.

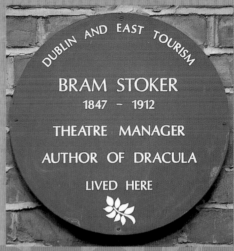

(1847–1912) and Sheridan Le Fanu (1814–73), who were both born in Dublin, took the lurid Gothic novel into the realms of literature. Le Fanu was the grand-nephew of Richard Brinsley Sheridan and the owner-editor of several Dublin journals, including the *Dublin Evening Mail* and the *Dublin University Magazine*. When his wife died in 1858, the grief-stricken journalist became a recluse, known to his friends as 'the Invisible Prince'. His most famous creations, *Uncle Silas* and *The House by the Churchyard*, were written in his bed between the hours of midnight and dawn in an effort to exorcise his increasing obsession with death and the supernatural.

In his youth, Bram Stoker was an avaricious reader of Le Fanu's short stories, and is said to have seized upon one in particular, *Carmilla*, as the inspiration for the bloodthirsty Count Dracula. Stoker began his career as the unpaid drama critic for the *Dublin Evening Mail*, but he did not stay at the paper long. His enthusiastic review of Sir Henry Irving's *Hamlet* led to a meeting with the great actor and an invitation to become Irving's business manager. *Dracula* was well received by the critics but sales were not sufficient to tempt Stoker to leave his day job with Irving. It was only with the popularity of Hamilton Deane's 1924 dramatization of the novel, long after Stoker's death, that the Count achieved lasting immortality.

ABOVE LEFT Photograph of Bram Stoker, author of the wonderfully gruesome Gothic horror story *Dracula*, taken c1900.

ABOVE Blue plaque marking Stoker's home in Kildare Street, Dublin.

OPPOSITE The inimitable Christopher Lee as Bram Stoker's bloodthirsty vampire, Count Dracula.

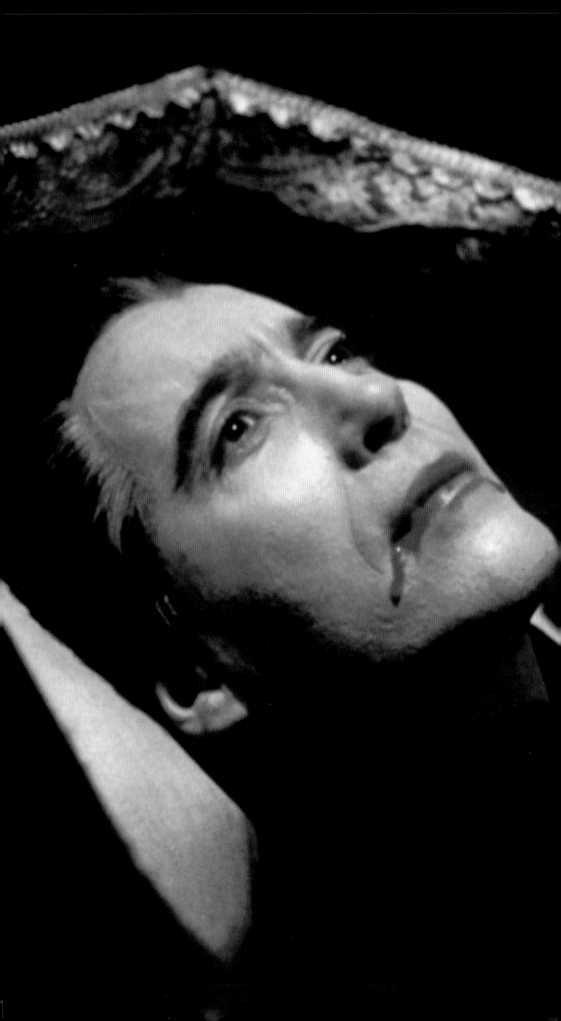

OSCAR

ABOVE Oscar Wilde, the Irish writer who continues to delight audiences with his wit in plays such as *The Importance of Being Earnest* and *Lady Windemere's Fan*.

OPPOSITE, LEFT A statue of one of Dublin's most famous sons, Oscar Wilde, in Merrion Square.

OPPOSITE, RIGHT Film still from the 1999 movie adaptation of Wilde's *An Ideal Husband*.

19TH-CENTURY DRAMA

More refined fare was to be had in the sophisticated social comedies of Oscar Wilde (1854–1900) and George Bernard Shaw (1856–1950), again both Dublin-born, whose work dominated the theatre on both sides of the Irish Sea from the 1880s until World War II.

Oscar's mother was the niece of the novelist Charles Robert Maturin and an enthusiastic nationalist. She wrote extensively on the nationalist cause, and consequently her salon became a meeting place for Dublin's literary elite, including Sheridan Le Fanu and the Greek scholar John Pentland Mahaffy ('the finest talker in Europe'), who was to become Wilde's mentor at Trinity. However, at the age of 20, Oscar declared himself in pursuit of 'beauty for beauty's sake' and left to find fame in England, initially as a writer of fiction with his only novel, the decadently stylish *The Picture of Dorian Gray*, and then with a series of witty drawing-room comedies including *Lady Windemere's Fan*, *A Woman of No Importance*, *An Ideal Husband* and *The Importance of Being Earnest*. His acerbic wit and calculated cynicism charmed the sophisticates, but neither his fame nor his ready repartee could save him from the wrath of the vindictive Marquis of Queensberry, who accused Oscar of sodomy and challenged Oscar to sue him for libel. The resulting court case witnessed Wilde broken and humiliated in public, after which he was prosecuted for being a homosexual and sentenced to two years hard labour.

ABOVE Dramatist George Bernard Shaw, c1900. Shaw achieved tremendous success outside Ireland, but many of his works were banned within his home country during his lifetime.

BELOW Shaw's bedroom in Synge Street, in the house where he was born, now preserved as a museum to the writer.

OPPOSITE Poster of *My Fair Lady*, the much-loved film adaptation of Shaw's *Pygmalion*, starring Audrey Hepburn and Rex Harrison.

He died a broken man in exile in France, where he had lived under the assumed name of Sebastian Melmoth, Maturin's haunted and immortal hero.

Shaw is said to have disliked Dublin and, at the age of 20, he eagerly followed his mother to London, where he attempted to make a living as a novelist. There he was introduced to the three passions of his later life: socialism, vegetarianism and the plays of Ibsen. Abandoning novels for social drama, he finally found success with his fourth play, *Arms and the Man*, which was warmly received on its opening night with one exception. A heckler brought the applause to a premature end and, in the embarrassing silence that followed, Shaw was heard to answer, 'I quite agree with you, but what can we two do against so many?'

By 1904 his reputation was firmly established in England, but he was effectively frozen out by his countrymen. W B Yeats rejected Shaw's satire *John Bull's Other Island* on behalf of the Irish Literary Theatre in Dublin, and the Lord Chamberlain of Ireland banned several Shaw plays on the grounds of either blasphemy or obscenity. *John Bull* was subsequently staged in London where Prime Minister Balfour saw it four times and King Edward Vll laughed so heartily that he broke his chair. Further stage successes were to make Shaw a celebrity throughout Europe and the United States, and led to his being awarded the Nobel Prize for Literature in 1925. These included *Man and Superman*, *Major Barbara*, *Saint Joan* and *Pygmalion*, plays whose philosophical and political aspects were intended to prick the audience's social conscience. The latter was later adapted as the musical comedy *My Fair Lady*.

A Shaw museum can be visited at his birthplace, 33 Synge Street, Dublin.

MARTIN & SOMERVILLE

THE NEW NOVELISTS:
LATE 19TH AND EARLY 20TH CENTURIES

The Irish comic novel was revived by Edith Somerville (1858–1949) and her writing partner Violet Florence Martin (1862–1915, writing under the pseudonym Martin Ross), who drew on their considerable knowledge of the hunting field for a trilogy of rural tales beginning with *Some Experiences of an Irish R.M.*, featuring a bemused English magistrate and his wily Irish nemesis Flurry Knox. During the authors' lifetimes, their books were widely recommended as a cure for quinsy, an inflammation of the tonsils that was thought to be alleviated by laughter. Almost a century later, they proved to have lost little of their charm when the stories were adapted for a television series.

In much the same vein were the comic novels of Percy French (1854–1920), who was also known for his music hall songs 'Abdallah Bubbul Ameer' and 'The Mountains Of Mourne', and those of George A Birmingham (1865–1950), a pseudonym of the Reverend J O Hannay, who proved adept at Swiftian satire.

A more natural narrative style was pioneered by the novelist George Moore (1852–1933), who was born in County Mayo and whose sojourn in Paris as a young man brought him into contact with Emile Zola. Moore's later work became more analytical as he absorbed the writings of Turgenev, whose influence could be discerned in a collection of short stories, *The Untilled Field*, and in his greatest novel, *Esther Waters*, the story of a young Irish servant girl who rebels against an oppressive environment. Moore's most accomplished work was the three volumes of memoirs of Irish literary life, published collectively as *Hail and Farewell*, in which he sketched scathing portraits of Yeats and members of Dublin high society, including a distinguished surgeon who boasted that his collection of antiques had been financed by specific operations.

GEORGE MOORE

OPPOSITE, LEFT
Photograph taken c1890
of Violet Florence Martin,
who wrote under the
pseudonym Martin Ross
in collaboration with her
cousin Edith Somerville.

OPPOSITE, RIGHT Irish
author Edith Somerville.
Her hilarious books,
written with her cousin,
were recommended as a
cure for quinsy, an
inflammation of the
tonsils that people
thought could be
alleviated by laughter.

ABOVE Drawing of the
novelist George Moore
by Edouard Manet.
Moore pioneered a more
natural narrative style
of writing in works such
as Hail and Farewell.

YEATS AND THE LITERARY REVIVAL

William Butler Yeats (1865–1939) captured the restless, yearning spirit of Irish nationalism in his plays and poetry, many of which are the finest ever written in the English language. A nominal member of the Irish Republican Brotherhood (a forerunner of the IRA) and a member of the Irish Free State Senate, Yeats glorified the nation's struggle for freedom in such plays as *Cathleen ni Houlihan* (in which his lifelong love Maud Gone took the title role) and in the elegy for those who sacrificed their lives in the Easter rising, *Easter 1916*, which contains the immortal line, 'All changed, changed utterly: A terrible beauty is born.'

His play *On Baile's Strand* was performed at the opening of the Abbey Theatre in 1904, where he served as a director to the end of his life, but it is on his poetry that his reputation rests and for which he was awarded the Nobel Prize for Literature in 1923.

Yeats's fellow director at the Abbey was the playwright John Millington Synge (1871–1909), whose use of idiomatic speech (a variation of Hiberno-English) and uncompromising realism in such plays as *In the Shadow of the Glen*, *Riders to the Sea* and *Playboy of the Western World* incurred the wrath of the romantics and the puritanical Dublin audience. The *Freeman's Journal* condemned the latter play as 'a libel upon Irish peasant men and, worse still, upon Irish girlhood', provoking organized riots at the Abbey whenever Synge's plays were staged.

Equally controversial were the plays of Padraic Colum (1881–1972), St John Ervine (1883–1971) and Lennox Robinson (1886–1958), who was at the forefront of a reform group known as 'the Cork Realists'. The shadow of Yeats threatened to obscure the careers of his friends and contemporaries, including the visionary poet George Russell (1867–1935), who wrote and painted under the name A E, and the prolific Katherine Tynan (1861–1931), who published 17 volumes of poetry and over 100 novels. However, a new generation of dramatists with a more strident voice were waiting impatiently in the wings.

OPPOSITE William Butler Yeats, the Nobel Prize-winning poet and dramatist who is perhaps Ireland's most distinguished literary figure.

ABOVE Barry Fitzgerald, Arthur Shields and Sara Allgood starring in the original theatrical production of John Millington Synge's *Playboy of the Western World.*

RIGHT Irish playwright John Millington Synge, painted by Jack Butler Yeats.

20TH-CENTURY DRAMA

Sean O'Casey (1880–1964) had left the Irish Citizen Army bitter and disillusioned two years before the Easter Uprising of 1916, and was determined to force his audiences to question the patriotic platitudes that had brought so much tragedy to their country. His first two plays, *The Shadow of a Gunman* and *Juno and the Paycock*, showed that the real victims of the civil war had been the civilians, while his third, *The Plough and the Stars*, bravely contrasted the reality of the uprising with the rhetoric that threatened to turn its heroic failure into myth. Such views proved too much for the Abbey audience, who rioted, provoking Yeats to castigate them with the words, 'You have disgraced yourselves again. Is this to be an ever recurring celebration of the arrival of Irish genius? Synge first and then O'Casey.'

In the aftermath, O'Casey chose voluntary exile in England, and thereafter his work lost the vigour and impact of his Dublin trilogy.

ABOVE Rehearsals at the Abbey Theatre in 1942 for Sean O'Casey's *The Plough and the Stars*.

OPPOSITE Irish playwright Sean O'Casey, whom W B Yeats hailed as one of Ireland's literary geniuses.

FOLLOWING PAGE Still from the movie adaptation of Roddy Doyle's acclaimed musical comedy/drama *The Commitments*.

ABOVE Milo O'Shea and
Barbara Jefford, playing
Bloom and Molly in a scene
from the film adaptation of
James Joyce's *Ulysses*.

JAMES JOYCE

Despite his misgivings concerning his fairness to the city of his birth, it was James Joyce (1882–1941) more than any other Irish writer who celebrated the character of the capital, the richness of its inhabitants and the musicality of their dialect in a collection of short stories, *The Dubliners*, and in the novels *A Portrait of the Artist as a Young Man* and *Ulysses*. In the latter, he adopted the conventions of a classical epic and the stylistic touches of an impressionist to describe one day in the life of his hero Leopold Bloom, who walks the streets of the city observing the minutiae of Dublin life and indulging in inner monologues that convey his thoughts and impressions. Every year on 16 June, fans of the writer make a literary pilgrimage to the city to visit the sites described in the book, beginning at the Martello Tower at Sandycove (now a Joyce museum) 13km (8 miles) from the centre of Dublin where the novel begins. A second museum is planned for 35 North Great George's Street.

Other notable Irish writers of the post-war period include Samuel Beckett, a friend of Joyce and a Nobel Prize-winning dramatist; Brendan Behan, who boasted of being thrown out of every pub in the capital; the Nobel Prize-winning poet Seamus Heaney; and popular novelists Molly Keane, Iris Murdoch, C S Lewis, Edna O'Brian, Maeve Binchy and Roddy Doyle. Each in their own way has immortalized an aspect of Ireland and the Irish character with its self-effacing humour, lilting speech and Joyce's unconventional beauty.

ABOVE Irish author James Joyce, 1938, whose Dublin-based novels capture the city's beauties and eccentricities.

FESTIVALS

Lord and Lady Shaftesbury at the Kildare Hunt Steeplechases in Punchestown, Dublin, on 22 April 1913. Horse racing still attracts large crowds of Dubliners, and, while the fashions have certainly changed, dressing to impress is still *de rigueur*.

& RELIGION
80–97

More than most European capitals, Dublin has been
transformed in recent years by economic growth and the
universal consumer culture that accompanies it. Not so
long ago a rather drab city, living on its Georgian past and
dominated by the distinctively puritanical spirit of Irish
Catholicism, Dublin has become a bustling place, consciously
European in outlook, full of enthusiasm and optimism, and
basking in the prestige and revenue brought by wine bars, discos,
arts centres and all the other impedimenta of big-city
sophistication. The Gaelic word *fleadh,* meaning festival, appears
everywhere, as new events are devised and old ones elaborated.

The new spirit has not always been easy to reconcile with long-established religious values, and indeed, the adjustment between the two is still going on. However, religion remains a vital part of many Dubliners' lives and a potent aspect of the national identity – part of the still-evolving synthesis that gives the city its special appeal.

Consumerism has yet to overcome Ireland's climate, and the early months of the year are quiet except for regular sporting fixtures such as the home matches of the Five Nations Rugby Tournament, held at the Landsdowne Road ground. The first international festival of the year takes place safely indoors from late February, when Dublin hosts a film festival that has steadily enhanced its international stature. However, the festival season only truly gets underway with the celebrations around and on St Patrick's Day – 17 March, the day on which the saint died in AD 462, and also, some say, the day on which he was born in about 389.

ST PATRICK'S DAY

Although St Patrick is Ireland's patron saint, he was not an Irishman. Born somewhere in the west of Roman Britain, at a time when the hard-pressed legions were no longer able to defend it effectively, Patrick was the son of a deacon and the grandson of a priest. The family was fairly prosperous, owning a villa from which Patrick was carried off by Irish pirates when he was about 16 years old. For six years he was a slave, serving a farmer in Ireland, until voices told him that he would soon be free and he managed to escape. After studying in Gaul, he was made a bishop and sent back to Ireland in AD 432. He was not the first Christian missionary in Ireland – a bishop named Palladius was already working in the south – but Patrick was evidently the most blessed or most charismatic figure in the field. He converted thousands, including the High King at Tara; drove the snakes from Ireland; and made the shamrock a personal and national symbol by using its trefoil shape to explain the oneness of the Trinity of Father, Son and Holy Ghost.

That, at any rate, is the Patrick of popular tradition. Scholars have long questioned many of the legends surrounding the saint, and recent research suggests that he lived about half a century later than had generally

ABOVE The 1999 Five Nations rugby match between Ireland and England. Despite Conor O'Shea's successful hurdling of an English tackler, Ireland lost the match 15 to 27.

OPPOSITE Religious painting by Giovanni Battista Tiepolo depicting St Patrick, c1740. St Patrick's Day on 17 March marks the beginning of Dublin's festival season.

Erin go Bragh

Hurrah for mother Erin, St Patrick's Day
For her sons and daughters scattered far away
For her harp and her emblem–the shamrock green
and for the best of all–her Irish Colleen.

been accepted. However, none of this has significantly affected the reverence in which he is held or the celebration of his feast day. The traditional celebrations were mainly domestic and low-key, although the shamrock was worn and 'drowning the shamrock' in whiskey was undertaken with a certain amount of ceremony. What now seems like the most familiar feature of a Dublin St Patrick's Day – the parade – is actually a recent development. Parades in the saint's honour were a 19th-century Irish-American invention, turning a religious festival into a robust assertion of Irish identity in a new and not always friendly land. Practised with ever-greater exuberance, parading remained an emigrant activity until the 1970s, when the first modest efforts were undertaken in Dublin. Mainly combining US marching bands led by drum majorettes with floats sponsored by local firms, the annual parade had a limited impact. Its popularity was not helped by the fact that the date was too early in the year to offer much hope of good weather, and in fact a cold, wet St Patrick's Day came to be seen as something of a Dublin tradition.

Nevertheless, the parade and attendant celebrations gradually became larger and more colourful. The 1990s witnessed a transformation in this as in other areas of Irish life, brought about by prosperity, enthusiasm for the European Union, design consciousness and the growth of the tourist industry. St Patrick's Day became a focus for a variety of other events. March music festivals proliferated as the long-established and classically oriented Feis Ceoil competition was joined by Celtic Flame and the booming, fashionable Temple Bar area staged its own St Patrick's music festival. During the same period, exhibitions, shows and street-theatre performances began to be timed to exploit the crowds that gathered to see the parade.

In 1998 this expansion was formally recognized by the inauguration of a four-day St Patrick's Festival. The 1999 event seemed likely to establish a pattern for the future, introduced by a 'Symphony of Fire' fireworks spectacular on the Saturday night, followed by three days of happenings and partying, when Cuban and African dancers vied with one another and Homer's *Odyssey* became the stuff of street theatre. It culminated on the

ABOVE Young shamrocks enjoying the St Patrick's Day parade in Dublin. Wearing the shamrock is a traditional part of the celebrations, but the original low-key approach has now been well and truly transformed into a festival extravaganza.

OPPOSITE Victorian postcard depicting a St Patrick's Day jig with accompanying verse.

ABOVE American marching band at the St Patrick's Day parade in Dublin.

saint's own day in a people-packed – and on this occasion sun-drenched – spectacle, most easily viewed by those who took part on stilts. Shamrocks were worn and the Liffey was dyed green, but the atmosphere was part-European, part-American, in line with Dublin's new sophistication. Typical of the eclectic spirit of the occasion was the way in which the traditionally genteel opening display of vintage cars was followed by a roaring fleet of Harley Davidson motorbikes, ridden by wild, leather-clad figures.

As in earlier years, the marching bands and mounted Gardai (police) were there, and the Lord Mayor passed in his 300-year-old coach, but the main parade was a flamboyant affair on a not-too-serious 'Heaven and Hell' theme, with interventions by salsa dancers. Splendidly grotesque floats and extravagantly dressed angels, demons and saints assembled at St Stephen's Green before weaving their way through streets cleared of traffic, past St Patrick's and Christ Church Cathedrals, over the river and through O'Connell Street to Parnell Square – when the music took over again with a ceilidh held in St Stephen's Green.

Not everyone approves of the way in which St Patrick's Day in Dublin has been expanded into a cosmopolitan festival. Local people in the crowds, feeling themselves heavily outnumbered, are apt to make remarks like 'It's a case of spot the Irishman', which reflect their ambivalent feelings about the transformation of the saint into a tourist attraction. The conflict between old and new values has appeared on a more serious level in objections voiced by some devout Catholics to a parade that honours the saint in name but, aside from a preliminary blessing, excludes any serious religious content and emphasizes the entertainment value of St Patrick associations. Controversy was especially fierce in 1998, when the theme was magic and wizardry. Outraged by this apparent endorsement of pagan practices, several hundred people protested by staging their own march, carrying crosses, religious statues and rosaries. Those who enjoyed the official parade felt that the magic and wizardry were no more than excuses for a little fun, and the carnival atmosphere was retained in 1999, albeit with the rather less contentious heaven-and-hell theme.

OPPOSITE Captain John Ledingham at the Dublin Horse Show, 1995. This event is just as much a social occasion as it is an opportunity to watch top-class equestrian displays.

BELOW One of the extravagant floats featuring in the modern, cosmopolitan St Patrick's Day parade, Dublin.

SUMMER SEASON

With little in the way of a pause, each
St Patrick's Day is followed by a summer
season of exhibitions, sporting events and
festivities, ranging from agricultural shows
to marathons. Feis Ceoil extends into April,
when crews from University College and
Trinity College contest the Colours Boat
Race along the Liffey. There is a national
holiday on 1 May, celebrated with parades,
after which the Dublin Garden Festival takes
place on the cusp of the sunniest months,
May and June. Summer in Dublin is
wonderful for the music lover, featuring
specialist festivals and many free concerts in
St Stephen's Green and other parks. In
August, the Dublin Horse Show is more than
a series of showjumping and dressage
competitions: many of the spectators are
there to be seen rather than to watch, offering
a Who's Who of Irish society and a What
Now of contemporary fashion. September
starts in non-sartorial vein with the Liffey
Swim, when the intrepid breast the river from
Watling Street Bridge to the Custom House
while crowds of the less intrepid derive
vicarious enjoyment from their efforts. The
Great Indoors beckons again in October,

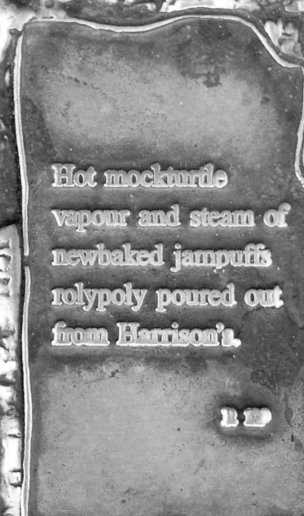

ULYSSES

Hot mockturtle vapour and steam of newbaked jampuffs rolypoly poured out from Harrison's.

C&C

proudly sponsored by
Cantrell & Cochrane (Dublin) Limited

when the season ends splendidly with a celebration of one of the great Irish arts, placed in a wider context by the fortnight-long Dublin Theatre Festival.

BLOOMSDAY

No other Dublin festival is remotely likely to equal St Patrick's as an international crowd-puller. However, in recent years an unquestioned second place has been taken by an event whose origin and significance are very different from the saint's day. Bloomsday, 16 June, is based on the events in a novel – James Joyce's masterpiece *Ulysses*, published in Paris in 1922 but long-banned throughout the English-speaking world. Though experimental in form and language, with an elaborate series of references to, among others, Homer and Shakespeare, *Ulysses* is at its most basic level a narrative of events taking place in Dublin on a single day, 16 June 1904. Joyce, though writing in self-chosen exile, took great pains to describe places and people just as they were during that period of less than 24 hours. (The date had a personal significance for him that played no part in the novel, since it was when he first walked out with the woman who was to share his life, Nora Barnacle.) *Ulysses* describes the wanderings through Dublin of its principal character, Leopold Bloom, an Irish Jew who is both an outsider figure and an ordinary man, and of the intellectual young artist Stephen Dedalus. Early in the book, Stephen leaves the Martello Tower on the shore at Sandycove where he is staying, and Bloom goes out of his house in Eccles Street. Their preoccupations take them all over the city, to school and cemetery, newspaper office and library, streets and beaches, the public house, the hospital and brothel, where they meet and briefly form a father-and-son-like relationship.

As a banned book, *Ulysses* was known in Dublin to only a handful of people, most of whom were writers. The first Bloomsday, 16 June 1954, was held to protest against censorship and involved writers such as Patrick Kavanagh and Flann O'Brien in a cross-city journey that by all accounts turned into a chaotic and acrimonious pub crawl. Publication of the novel in Ireland came in the 1960s, and later a more liberal Dublin learned to admire Joyce, as well as appreciate

OPPOSITE Bloomsday plaque on one of the sites referred to in James Joyce's *Ulysses*. The Bloomsday festival involves following the steps of Joyce's protagonists through the city of Dublin.

BELOW The Martello Tower at Sandycove, where Dublin's Bloomsday pilgrimage begins on 16 June each year.

his usefulness as a tourist attraction. By the 1990s, there were Joyce museums in the Sandycove Martello Tower and at the James Joyce Centre in North Great George's Street, a Georgian house that figured in *Ulysses* as the place where Denis J Maginni held dancing classes. Joyce himself was honoured with a statue in Earl Street North. Bloomsday was celebrated by readings and enactments at these and other points on the Bloom-Dedalus itinerary. Those who turned out for the event wore cycling caps, boaters and other items representing the fashions of 1904, and the more literary-minded began the day at Sandycove with a 'Joyce breakfast' of kidneys and Guinness, and lunched, like Bloom, on a gorgonzola sandwich and a glass of burgundy at Davy Byrne's pub in Duke Street.

With the approach of the millennium, purists became increasingly concerned as Bloomsday turned into a commercialized Edwardian jamboree, complete with another pageant of vintage cars, instead of a literary pilgrimage. Like St Patrick's Day, it expanded and lost something of its original identity, becoming a week-long festival, effectively incorporating other events such as the Belfast–Dublin cycle marathon (Maracycle) and featuring a multitude of dubiously Joyce-themed excursions, offers and memorabilia. The carnival atmosphere of the contemporary Bloomsday has caused qualms even among those who benefit financially, such as the Joyce Centre, and in 1998 caused the Nobel Prize-winning Irish poet Seamus Heaney to abandon the proceedings and leave Dublin in disgust. However, it cannot be said that Joyce's actual work has been forgotten in the razzmatazz. Dublin's love affair with modernity led to what must have been the novel's widest public exposure, a 14-hour reading of the entire text of *Ulysses* over the internet, with the participation in Dublin of the Irish president, Mary McAleese, and the well-known novelist Edna O'Brien.

THE ROLE OF RELIGION

Dublin's festivals may have an unmistakably secular flavour, but religion remains ever-present in the city's fabric and still looms large in everyday life. The overwhelming majority of Dubliners have been brought up in the Roman Catholic faith, and although church attendance has fallen – especially

TOP Statue of James Joyce in Earl Street North, Dublin.

ABOVE Pilgrims climbing Croagh Patrick in County Mayo as part of the religious observances marking Lent.

among the young – religious observance is still very high by European standards. The influence of the Church in secular matters has declined sharply in recent years, partly because of scandals involving the clergy, and partly as a result of the impact of modern urban and consumerist values on Ireland's no longer enclosed society. Dubliners have taken notably liberal attitudes on contentious issues such as divorce, contraception and abortion, and outward signs of devotion, such as making the sign of the cross when passing a church, are much less in evidence than a few years ago. However, respect for the Church remains strong among the lapsed as well as the faithful. Occasions such as Lent are taken as seriously as ever, and Dubliners are to be found among the pilgrims to Croagh Patrick and other sites. Hospitals, schools and other

ABOVE A beautiful, richly coloured stained-glass window in Christ Church Cathedral, Dublin.

FOLLOWING PAGE Christ Church Cathedral was the first stone building in Dublin. Built by the Normans on the site of an older wooden building, the cathedral was restored in the 19th century with a number of Gothic additions.

institutions are still largely staffed and run by the Church, and priests and members of the religious orders remain familiar sights on the streets of Dublin.

Only very small numbers of Dubliners are non-Catholics, although both Protestants and Jews have made important contributions to the city's history. One curious hangover from the past is the fact that most of Dublin's venerable ecclesiastical buildings, including the city's two cathedrals, St Patrick's and Christ Church, are not Catholic properties but belong to the Church of Ireland. For over three centuries, from the time of the 16th-century Reformation in England, the Church of Ireland was the established national church, like its sister-denomination across the Irish Sea, the Church of England;. Among other things, it took over the country's churches and cathedrals, so that when Catholics were granted freedom of worship they had to start again and put up their own religious edifices.

Unlike the Church of England, the Church of Ireland never commanded mass support, functioning as the church of the Protestant ruling class, often called the Anglo-Irish or the Ascendancy, which dominated Irish society until British rule came to an end. The wealth and power of the Ascendancy were founded on injustices done to the Catholic minority. However, it must also be said that many great Irish figures sprang from the Anglo-Irish, including patriotic leaders such as Wolfe Tone and Charles Stewart Parnell, and a host of writers from Swift and Sheridan to W B Yeats and George Bernard Shaw.

Jonathan Swift, author of *Gulliver's Travels*, was the dean of St Patrick's from 1713 until his death in 1745. The cathedral contains his death-mask and items linked with his life and work. Swift himself is buried there. Among other notable people memorialized in St Patrick's is the harpist Turlough Carolan, 'the last of the bards', and Douglas Hyde, pioneer revivalist of the Gaelic language and president of Eire (1938–45). Objects preserved in the cathedral include an old door with a hole in it whose history may serve as an antidote to over-idealized views of medieval religious life. In 1492, a brawl broke out in St Patrick's between rival magnates Kildare and Ormonde and their followers. Ormonde and

BELOW The towering nave of St Patrick's Cathedral with its high, vaulted arches is named in honour of Ireland's patron saint.

his men got the worse of it and barricaded themselves in the chapterhouse. Efforts to make peace were successful, and a hole was cut into the door. Kildare then thrust his hand through the hole to shake Ormonde's hand, a piece of risk-taking that is said to have given rise to the phrase 'chancing your arm'.

Both Christ Church and St Patrick's are ancient foundations, although as stone buildings they date back only to the 12th century. Christ Church is the older, built from 1172 with the support of Strongbow, the Anglo-Norman baron whose success in carving out a great lordship sparked off the long history of English attempts to dominate Ireland. St Patrick's was founded in 1191, just outside the city walls so that Christ Church could not claim jurisdiction over it. One of the prime movers was a certain Henri de Londres, who had quarrelled with the Christ Church authorities, and rivalry between the two foundations persisted down the ages.

St Patrick's was eventually recognized as the national cathedral of the Church of Ireland, and it also became (and remains) the largest church in the entire country. Like Christ Church, it is now essentially a 19th-century Gothic building, internally less beautiful than its rival but providing a spectacular setting for services, and in particular, because of its size and excellent acoustics, for choir recitals. St Patrick's choir school has a long history: it was founded in 1432, and its members took part in the first-ever performance of Handel's *Messiah* in Fishamble Street on 13 April 1742. The anniversary of this momentous occasion is currently celebrated every year in Dublin by Our Lady's Choral Society, who stand on the spot at noon and sing a selection of choruses from the oratorio. Still justly admired, the red-frocked choristers of St Patrick's perform in public, six days a week, every July and August, when they attract appreciative audiences of various nationalities and faiths.

Other Protestant churches in Dublin include St Werburgh's, reputedly the burial place of cockle-and-mussel-selling Molly Malone and certainly the last resting-place of Lord Edward Fitzgerald, the best-known leader of the 1798 rebellion; St Audoen's, the city's earliest surviving medieval church; and St Michan's, famous for the amazingly

TOP St Patrick's Cathedral was virtually rebuilt in the 19th century, though it originally dates to 1191.

ABOVE Plaque erected in memory of Turlough Carolan in St Patrick's Cathedral. Sponsored by novelist Lady Morgan.

well-preserved corpses in its vaults, where a combination of limestone and methane seem to have created the driest spot in Ireland.

Catholic churches and other ecclesiastical buildings are far more numerous but less distinguished, having been raised in the 19th century, often as a grudging concession by the Anglo-Irish ruling class. Consequently, St Mary's Pro-Cathedral stands in rather an out-of-the-way position behind the main O'Connell Street thoroughfare, on Marlborough Street. Its Palestrina Choir rivals that of St Patrick's, performing at mass every Sunday morning.

Believers and non-believers alike celebrate the final days of the year, whether enjoying the run-up to Christmas with pagan abandon or fasting on Christmas Eve before attending midnight mass. After the pleasures of Christmas Day, on St Stephen's Day, 26 December, boys dressed as chimney sweeps ('Wren boys') go round singing hymns to raise money for charity. On 31 December, Dubliners join in the worldwide merrymaking that sees out the old year, with regret or relief, and welcomes in the new.

OPPOSITE A Victorian Christmas card. Dubliners celebrate Christmas in many ways, both with pagan abandon and with religous reverence.

BELOW Mummified remains in the Protestant church of St Michan's in Church Street, Dublin. Their remarkable state of preservation is due to the dry atmosphere created by a combination of limestone and methane.

MERRY CHRISTMAS

Text: Clare Connery

FOOD & DRI
98—121

NK

A delivery of Guinness in Marlborough Street, Dublin.
This world-famous black stout has become one of
Ireland's national emblems, and is a source of both
pride and pleasure to the people of Dublin.

Somewhere in the dim and distant past, Ireland lost sight of the abundance, variety and quality of the food within its midst. So much so, in fact, that until recently the idea of Irish food being talked about, written about and hailed as something 'great' would have been laughed at by most of Ireland's inhabitants. Indeed, the very notion that a 'national' cuisine even existed would not have entered anyone's head. As a nation, the Irish have never been ones to shout about their assets or talents – on the contrary, they have always been much more ready to do themselves down, knocking their own in deference to someone else's. Indeed, in the case of food products and eating traditions, up until about 20 years ago, the majority of Irish people probably never understood or appreciated them. What they did believe, however, was that food from almost every country in the world was far superior to anything Ireland could produce. Consequently, Irish food and cooking, either intentionally or not, has been one of Ireland's best-kept secrets.

OPPOSITE Guinness being served in Ryans Bar, Dublin. The drink is famed for its creamy head, smooth taste and the length of time it takes to pull the perfect pint.

ABOVE Oysters and Guinness, a favourite combination in Dublin's pubs and restaurants.

BELOW Cavistons Seafood Restaurant in Sandycove serves some of the best fish dishes in Dublin.

Fortunately, things have changed. Ireland has come of age and now has the self-confidence both to be proud of and appreciate its rich culinary heritage, as well as the glorious bounty that is to be found on land, sea and shore. Once more, Ireland is being regarded as a 'land of milk and honey', and its culinary traditions to be of considerable value.

Traditional Irish cooking is the cooking of an agricultural society created by an unpretentious and unsophisticated people, who considered the main purpose of food to be to nourish and sustain rather than to titillate. Some might describe it as 'peasant cooking'. Whatever, Irish cooking has evolved over many hundreds of years, and is part and parcel of the country's history, mythology, folklore and legend. It is partly the legacy of famine, poverty and harsh circumstances, but also the result of a varied and fertile landscape. Today, as in the past, beef, lamb, pork, poultry, game, fish and dairy produce form the backbone of the Irish table, along with a well-stocked basket of vegetables and fruit. With these, a simple but wholesome cuisine of soups and stewed, roasted, braised and fried dishes were created along with a wide range of breads, cakes and puddings.

THE IRISH TABLE:
FOOD INFLUENCES AND DEVELOPMENTS

The best examples of Irish cooking have generally been in the demesne of the family home rather than the pub, hotel or restaurant. As a result, although Ireland has always been renowned for its ladened tables and generous hospitality, the finer elements of Irish cooking have more often than not remained illusive to the passing traveller. This in turn has given rise to the common

ABOVE Dublin coddle combines potatoes, ham and sausages to make a warm and hearty dish, perfect for Dublin's cold winter nights.

OPPOSITE Café Java, one of the many coffee houses that abound in Dublin.

perception that Irish food is dull, monotonous, badly cooked and unimaginative, with the emphasis on quantity rather than quality. Indeed, Ireland over the years has become stereotyped as the land of the potato, Irish stew, boiled bacon and cabbage and, of course, whiskey and Guinness. This is not altogether untrue, but it is only a small part of a much more interesting culinary patchwork.

In recent years, enormous changes have taken place on the Irish food scene. A little band of pioneer 'foodies' who appreciate Ireland's food heritage and quality produce have dedicated themselves not only to spreading the word about the treasures on Ireland's doorstep, but also to putting into practice the gospel they preach in their own restaurants, pubs and hotels. They have sung the praises of Irish food at every possible opportunity through the length and breadth of the country.

For the last 30 years, chefs like John Howard of Le Coq Hardi in Dublin and Gerry Galvin of Drimcong House in County Galway, led by the famous Myrtle Allen of Ballamaloe House in County Cork, have been undeterred, battling away, encouraging, teaching and influencing. They have not only re-established Ireland's culinary heritage but also enlightened a whole nation. Along with the parallel influences from Europe, Asia and the United States, these Irish prophets have inspired a new generation of talented young chefs, who are now not only renowned in Ireland but can hold their own on the international stage. It is these stalwarts that have helped facilitate the creation of what is today being hailed as 'modern Irish cuisine'.

NEW IRISH CUISINE

The new Irish cuisine favours the use of indigenous Irish products and uses them with pride, but is equally happy to combine them with specialty produce from other countries. It is a cuisine that is no longer afraid of its 'roots', but uses the influence of tradition as a basis on which to develop and create an altogether lighter, more aesthetically beautiful style of cooking. It is a relaxed cuisine, free from rigid constraints, and has allowed the talents of young chefs like Kevin Thornton, Conrad Gallagher and Derry Clarke to develop unfettered. Traditional and modern

In fact, in Dublin the trends in food and drink are following a similar pattern to those in the rest of Europe, but on a much smaller scale. Eating out has become the national pastime, fuelled by a young affluent society that wants to eat out, eat in, entertain, be entertained and generally enjoy themselves. There has literally been a culinary explosion: cooking has become trendy, chefs celebrities, and food is very fashionable.

The Dublin of today is modern, cosmopolitan and vibrant, and this is reflected in its vast array of bistros, cafés, brasseries, pubs and restaurants. There is something in Dublin for every pocket, taste and time of day. In fact, in whatever part of Dublin you find yourself, whether it is the city centre, the north side, the south side or the sprawling outskirts, a gem of an eating place is there to be found.

THE DUBLIN RESTAURANT SCENE

It is in Dublin that some of the greatest gastronomic experiences in the whole of Ireland can be enjoyed, created both by chefs and restaurateurs of wisdom and experience and by brash young talent set to overturn convention. One of the most celebrated and influential of the old school is John Howard, chef/proprietor of Le Coq Hardi in Pembroke Road, Ballsbridge. Since 1977, he has blended his distinguished French cooking with a love of his native Irish to create some of the best food on the island and a perfect example of new Irish cuisine. His wine list, too, is considered to be one of the finest in the country.

Patrick Guilbaud, also a veteran of the Dublin restaurant scene, has been waving his culinary wand in the city for the past 17 years – long enough to be classed as an honorary Irishman! He also combines the best of Irish produce with Gallic flair and inspiration. In the wonderful setting of his restaurant in the Main House of the Merrion Hotel in Upper Merrion Street, along with his head chef Guillaume Le Brun, Guilbaud has created a classic dining experience that is both elegant and relaxed.

Another well-established restaurant on the Dublin food trail, noted for its consistently good stylish food and warm convivial atmosphere, is Dobbins, situated since its inception in 1978 in a rather unlikely lane

rest comfortably together, and provide consumers with an enviable choice – there is certainly room for them both.

The surge of culinary re-awakening and creativity sweeping throughout the country is not just confined to the ' new Irish cuisine ' or the big cities. Fine food and fine talents of all kinds are to be found everywhere, even in the most far-flung places, delighting the locals and frequently surprising the traveller. However, as with any major development, the main surge of activity is concentrated on the cities, and in this, Dublin has been at the forefront. It is in Dublin that you will find a touch of everything – a cornucopia of colours, flavours and textures. There is something for all tastes and nationalities crammed into what is a relatively small city. Mediterranean styles compete with cooking from the Pacific Rim, the many different cuisines of Asia jostle with those from the New World, and there is Fusion everywhere.

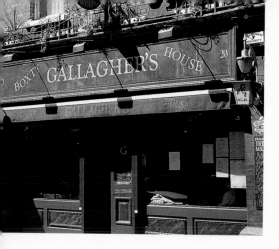

not far from Merrion Square, in an equally unlikely building. Here, restaurateur John O'Byrne and chef Gary Flynn have provided both loyal customers and visitors with one of the city's best eating-out experiences.

Just around the corner is L'Ecrivan, within walking distance of St Stephen's Green. Here, another Irish star, the talented chef/owner Derry Clarke, has created a multifaceted series of menus with French, Mediterranean and strong Irish influences in a variety of price ranges.

Not a stone's throw away in Ballsbridge is another of Dublin's institutions, and one of Ireland's busiest and best-loved restaurants, Roly's Bistro. Here, in a lively, bustling atmosphere, one of Ireland's most highly regarded chefs and part-owner of the bistro, Colin O' Daly, has created a menu that, although influenced by both France and Ireland, also encapsulates the mood of the moment in the wider world. Over the years, Roly's seems to have achieved just the right balance of informality and sophistication, and all at an affordable price. So much so, in fact, that the formula has been exported to Palm Beach, Florida.

There are a number of other fine restaurants in Dublin with a strong French influence, but the two paramount are Les Frères Jacques and La Mère Zou. Les Frères Jacques in Dame Street in the Temple Bar area of the city has been going since 1986, and is totally French-owned and run. The menu is distinctly French, with a strong emphasis on fish. La Mère Zou opened in 1994 not far from the Shelbourne Hotel in St Stephen's Green, and concentrates on French country-style cooking.

In contrast, La Stampa in Dawson Street is the place to eat in grand style. Here, the atmosphere is reminiscent of continental high life at the turn of the century. The dining room is one of Ireland's most beautiful, and it is certainly the place to go for fine food and fun. The menu has an Italian/ Mediterranean feel and offers plenty of choice.

One of Dublin's most well-known, flamboyant and controversial chef/restaurateurs is Conrad Gallagher, who continues to infuse flavours, colours and styles at his restaurant Peacock Alley in the recently opened Fitzwilliam Hotel on St Stephen's Green. Here, he practises his art on two levels, in the main Restaurant Conrad Gallagher at the Fitzwilliam Hotel, close to the roof garden, and in Christopher's, a brasserie-style eatery on the mezzanine floor. The style of food is also on two levels, literally reaching the heights in the upper echelons, while equally good but much less studied on the lower plain. In Conrad Gallagher's Lloyds Brasserie in Merrion Street Upper, he has a similarly stylish but much more casual restaurant serving trendy but excellent modern food.

If Conrad Gallagher is one of Ireland's more high-profile chefs, Kevin Thornton could be described as one of Ireland's more modest and discrete leading lights, considered by many to be the best young chef in the country. In an unpretentious corner building overlooking Dublin's Grand Canal in Portabello, where the decor is simple and understated, the service first-class and the cooking of the chef/proprietor nothing less than superb, you will have an unforgettable experience. No gastronomic pilgrimage to Dublin would be complete without a visit.

If fish is your passion, then there are a number of restaurants where fish is the main feature on the menu. The Lord Edward in

ABOVE The Fitzwilliam Hotel on St Stephen's Green, where chef Conrad Gallagher has two of his restaurants.

OPPOSITE Boulevard Café on Exchequer Street, a trendy haven after a day shopping.

Christchurch Place, overlooking the cathedral, is Dublin's oldest. Cavistons Seafood Restaurant, behind the seafront in Dun Laoghaire, just south of the city centre, serves an imaginative selection of seafood dishes in the restaurant section of the best fish shop and delicatessen in the whole of Dublin. Also in Dun Laoghaire is Brasserie Na Mara, an attractive harbour-side restaurant in a fine old building. On the north side of the city on Howth Pier is the long-established King Sitric Fish Restaurant, where the menu changes daily, depending on the day's catch.

CAFE SOCIETY

On a completely different level, Dublin is right up there with other major cities for its trendy international café society. Here, all is buzz and chatter, the food fast and fashionable, and the drinks as likely to be a double café latté as a glass of wine. One is spoilt for choice. Right in the heart of the city on the south side of the River Liffey, in an area bordered by Trinity College, St Stephen's Green and Dublin Castle are some of the most fashionable meeting-eating places in the city. In Temple Bar, which has undergone a metamorphosis in recent years and now has the atmosphere of a mini-Covent Garden, you will be spoilt for choice, though you

ABOVE The Bad Ass Café, always packed out, is a mecca for the trendy young things of Dublin.

ABOVE Gotham Café, just off Grafton Street, is a good place to relax in an informal atmosphere.

might find that the surroundings and atmosphere are more enticing than the food. For quality, there is Fitzers Café, overlooking the central square; then there's the ever-trendy Bad Ass Café, a mecca for the young and the young at heart. It is always packed and buzzing; burgers, pizza, pasta and Mexican specialities are the main features. At the Mermaid Café, on the edge of Temple Bar, the cooking is stylish American in inspiration and the atmosphere less frenetic. The trend for mass kitchen warehouse eating that has flooded London has arrived in Dublin in the shape of Belgo. It is here that the young and trendy meet to eat.

Dawson Street boasts Café en Seine, the archetypal continental-style, high-ceilinged, long-mirrored bar/café, with lots of smokey atmosphere. A place to meet rather than eat and the Gotham Café just off Grafton Street serves good, light, informal food. However, it is Cooks Café in South William Street that still rides the crest of the wave of stylish cafés in this area, with lots of atmosphere and good Mediterranean food.

The Kilkenny Restaurant Café just opposite Trinity College is one of the more traditional café/restaurants, which for years has been a resting place for many a weary

ABOVE Bewley's Oriental Café on Grafton Street is Dublin's original coffee house, and is just as popular today as when it first appeared.

LEFT Bewley's combined restaurant and shop means that you can sample the food, then buy it to take home!

OPPOSITE Butlers Chocolate Café sells continental-style chocolate and coffee drinks as well as the divine Irish chocolates that are a treat for all tastebuds.

shopper. The food is homely, high quality and delicious. Bewley's is the original Dublin café/coffee house. It always seems to have been there, and is still a popular place to have a quick coffee and a bun. One of the most recent additions is Butlers Chocolate Café, a small, elegant chocolate bar where you can enjoy continental-style chocolate and coffee drinks while watching the customers queue at the counter to buy luxury Irish chocolates.

Just beyond the centre in fashionable Ballsbridge are a clutch of 'of the moment' café/bars. Coopers Café, with its eye-catching glass façade, serves international cuisine. Directly opposite, on the Royal Dublin Society's premises, is Fitzers Ballsbridge Café, where the food portrays a fusion of many different styles. Closer to the city centre, just off Pembroke Road, the Expresso Bar Café serves excellent Californian/Italian food in 'with-it' minimalist surroundings.

COSMOPOLITAN DUBLIN

If you want to be more 'ethnic' in Dublin, you will be able to enjoy the cuisines of India, China, Malaysia, Indonesia, Japan and Thailand throughout the city. The Eastern Tandoori in William Street and the Rajdoot in Clarendon Street were two of the first established, and have maintained their reputation for good food and service. Saagar in Harcourt Street is authentic in food and atmosphere. The Furma in Donnybrook and the Imperial in Wicklow Street are China's leading lights, and the Good World in South St George's Street is noted for Dim Sum. The Langkawi in Upper Baggot Street offers a combination of both Indian and Chinese cuisine, but specializes in dishes from Malaysia. At the Ayumi-Ya in Blackrock you will experience classic Japanese food, and The Chilli Club in Annes Lane is the first authentic Thai restaurant. After a slow start, Dublin is feeling the ethnic food surge.

BUDGET FOOD

Dublin offers a great variety of budget and fast-food alternatives, as in other major cities, from pasta and pizza to the ever-popular burger. However, still the favourite with Dubliners and visitors alike is the humble plate of fish and chips. The best-known establishment is Leo Burdock's in Werburgh Street, a landmark where there will be a queue at most times of the day.

ABOVE Leo Burdock's traditional fish and chip shop, established 1913, is a landmark on the streets of Dublin.

LEFT Abrakebabra, serving Dubliners with 'magic food' and 'super service'.

DUBLIN PUBS

While Dublin's international restaurant renown is a recent phenomenon, it is in the pubs – both ancient watering holes and modern emporia – that the grizzled, hard-bitten or smooth and elegant character of the city can be found. Here, Dubliners and visitors relax, have fun, soak up the atmosphere, see and be seen, and put the world to rights. Tongues are loosened 'to be sure' over 'a pint or two' of the black stuff, 'a snifter or two' of the hard stuff, or whatever concoction is in vogue with the spritzer set.

However, man (and woman) cannot live on the blackstuff (Guinness) alone, and in recent years, food has played an increasingly important part of the welcome in the city's traditional pubs. Consistent quality is not available in every establishment; you still have to be 'picky'. Side-by-side with the 'you could be anywhere' sandwiches, quiches, lasagne and salads, you will find time-honoured Irish classics. Look out for smoked salmon and wheaten bread, Dublin Bay prawns, oysters, Irish stew, beef in Guinness, and sausages and champ and, if you are lucky, Dublin's very own coddle – a plate of sausages, bacon and potatoes – which, at its best, is a truly delicious dish. The pub is an Irish institution, and there are literally hundreds in Dublin. Here is just a 'snifter' of what is on offer.

Davy Byrnes of Duke Street (just off Grafton Street) is still a popular call for

ABOVE Exterior of the Davy Byrnes pub, which is mentioned in James Joyce's masterwork *Ulysses*, is popular with both tourists and locals.

RIGHT Interior of the Davy Byrnes pub. Though recently refurbished, it still retains its original atmosphere and continues to pull in the punters.

ABOVE The Temple Bar, established 1840. As usual in Dublin's many public houses, Guinness – 'the emperor of malted liquors' – is served here.

OPPOSITE The Brazen Head is Ireland's oldest pub, established 1198.

FOLLOWING PAGE A traditional pub mirror with bottles of spirits lined in front of it, in Toner's, reputedly the only pub ever visited by W B Yeats.

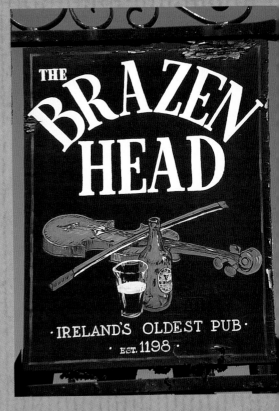

tourists and loyal regulars; though recently refurbished, it still has some of its old atmosphere. It is steeped in history and is mentioned in James Joyce's *Ulysses*. The Old Stand in Exchequer Street also oozes tradition. The Long Hall in South Great George's Street draws you in with its ornate façade; Toner's in Lower Baggot Street is said to be the only pub ever visited by W B Yeats; and the nearby 18th-century Brazen Head is perhaps the most authentic old pub in the city. Three genuine Victorian establishments with oodles of atmosphere and original features are Ryans of Park Gate Street, Kavanaghs of Glasneven and The Stag's Head in Dame Court.

Temple Bar, Dublin's South Bank, is the place to go for razzmatazz and atmosphere, and literally every other building houses a pub or eatery. There will always be a crush to get into The Temple Bar, The Auld Dubliner, The Quays and The Norseman, but the most popular is The Oliver St John Gogarty in Fleet Street. Here, they really do have to shoe horn them in. There is traditional live music and an authentic Irish menu. The most 'swish' in the area is the Octagon Bar at the Clarence Hotel, owned by members of the rock band U2.

Of the new breed of traditional theme pubs, The Porterhouse in Parliament Street is worth a visit. It is Ireland's first microbrewery, with 10 award-winning ales brewed on the premises, and is a happy combination of traditional and modern.

Since there is a pub around every corner in Dublin, follow your nose and instinct – at the very least, the Guinness will be good!

DUBLIN'S FOOD AND WINE SHOPS AND MARKETS

As 'eating out' has become more discerning and adventurous, so has 'eating in' at home. In response to Dublin's growing international perspective, food shops, delicatessens and superstores stock an ever-wider range of cosmopolitan foodstuffs. Dublin's 'foodies', although not nearly as well-served as their counterparts in London, Paris or Rome, can nonetheless ferret out what they need in specialist shops. For fruit and vegetables, there is an excellent selection at Roy Foxes of Donnybrook, most of the major supermarkets, and for the early bird a trip to the wholesale fruit and vegetable market at Smithfield. For fish, Thomas Mulloy and McConnell's just off Grafton Street serve the city well, but a jaunt out to Howth Harbour

such as Findlater's in the Harcourt Street Vaults, Mitchell & Son of Kildare Street, and McCabe's of Blackrock, will tempt you with their wares. On a slightly different, but no less acceptable, level, the supermarkets have also developed excellent, keenly priced selections. In all these emporiums, of course, there will be a notable selection of indigenous beverages, from sparkling waters, beers, ales to porters, stouts and whiskeys. Two of Irelands most famous exports, Guinness and Jamesons Whiskey, are produced in Dublin, and both offer tours and tastings.

north of the city or Dun Laoghaire in the south will assure you of the finest and the freshest. There are many butchers throughout the city, but reputedly the finest is Hick's Butchers at Sallynoggin. For a delicious range of both Irish and continental-type breads, it is hard to beat Cooke's Bakery in Francis Street and the Bretzel Kosher Bakery in Lennox Street. The bread from both these bakeries is also to be found in many delicatessens around the city. Just off Grafton Street, Sheridans has the most perfect range of fine speciality cheeses in the country, all displayed in a beautifully designed, temperature-controlled shop. Little Italy in North King Street, near Smithfield Market, is a must for all things Italian; The Asia Market in Drury street for all things Asian; and Aya in Clarendon Street, just beside Brown and Thomas, for all things Japanese. By far the best all-round food shop/delicatessen, however, is Cavistons Delicatessen at Sandycove. Here, the discerning shopper will find fresh fish, fruit and vegetables, cheese, cooked meats, readymade meals, bread, chocolates and a full range of groceries, in an atmosphere-packed Aladdin's cave. The Saturday market in Meeting House Square in the heart of Temple Bar has a number of food stalls selling top-quality produce, and is a good place to go to find something a little bit different.

To help all this food go down, a number of specialist wine merchants of long standing,

TOP A selection of Irish cheeses on sale at the Big Cheese Company.

ABOVE Mitchells wine merchants on Kildare Street has a long-standing reputation as a purveyor of fine wines and spirits.

OPPOSITE A fishmonger at Moore Street Market, which is famed for the cacophonous women who ply their wares there.

Riverdance, here featuring its original star Michael Flaherty, set the world alight with a passion for all things Irish. With its modern take on a traditional dance form, audiences around the world became devoted fans of Irish music, dance, flair and style.

Text: David Sandison

MUSIC
122-145

There is a greater chance, it has been said, of spending a day in Dublin (or anywhere in Ireland, for that matter) without experiencing a spot of rain than there is of not hearing someone, somewhere, playing music. It may be no more than a lone fiddler, guitarist or tin-whistle player on a street corner, but there will always be music of some variety. These days, it is more likely to be the sounds of a folk, rock or jazz group that you will hear escaping from the doors and windows of pubs or clubs, but you will hear it. The Irish, you see, simply love to make music. It's in the blood.

A TOUCH OF TECHNICOLOR

The Irish passion for making music is as old as history itself, and has been recorded by many observers. A passage from James Joyce's 1916 novel *A Portrait of the Artist as a Young Man*, for example, describes the merry wheeze of a concertina being played and its miraculous effect on those who hear it: '… Stephen passed out on to the wide platform above the steps and was conscious of the caress of mild evening air. Towards Findlater's church a quartet of young men were striding along with linked arms, swaying their heads and stepping to the agile melody of their leader's concertina. The music passed in an instant, as the first bars of sudden music always did, over the fantastic fabrics of his mind, dissolving them painlessly and noiselessly as a sudden wave dissolves the sand-built turrets of children.'

Time was, way back in their myth- and legend-wreathed past, when the Irish used music and song to help preserve their history and recount tales of heroes, villains, magic, mystery and great battles. Like other Celtic tribes, theirs was an oral tradition, with nothing written down. That being so, melodies and verse provided a dash of Technicolor to make those stories even more memorable as they were handed on to the next generation.

AN ARSENAL OF INSTRUMENTS

In common with most prehistoric societies, the Irish Celts initially used only drums to support those songs, settling on the bodhrán (pronounced 'boran') – a one-sided tambourine-like goatskin drum beaten with a single stick or fingers – as early as the late

TOP *Gypsy Caravan* by William Mulready, 19th century. The poster in the painting implores 'Come and see wonderful performing dog'.

ABOVE A fiddle, guitar and accordian trio is a common sight in Dublin's pubs.

OPPOSITE The Irish one-sided bodhrán drum.

ABOVE Christy Moore playing the Irish bodhrán drum, which can be played both with a stick and with the fingers.

OPPOSITE The harp became popular in Ireland from the second half of the first millennium, and featured on the very first coins minted in the country in the 13th century.

Bronze Age. The bodhrán's survival, and its continued importance at the core of modern Irish folk music, owes everything to the brilliance of those who are able to create bewilderingly complex patterns of sound from those stretched hides.

A combination of natural inventiveness, travel and trade led to the gradual introduction of other instruments down the centuries. Chief among these, certainly during the second half of the first millennium, was the harp. It is no coincidence that the first coins minted in Ireland in the 13th century featured a harp motif, nor that modern Ireland's national emblem is the harp, for harpers were the superstars of Irish society between the 10th and 17th centuries, enjoying high status, privilege and the patronage of clan chiefs. It would not be until the early 19th century, however, that a notation of traditional Irish harp music was collected and published by the archivist Edward Bunting as *The Ancient Music of Ireland.*

Chief among the instruments that were taken up by Irish musicians down the years, and that helped to create a distinctively Celtic 'voice', were flutes and whistles, the uillean pipes and the fiddle, each of which was also given a particular local styling. Thus, the trained ear can easily discern whether a fiddle player hails from Donegal, for example, or from Kerry, Cork or Sligo. The overwhelming dominance of the Sligo style of playing is due in no small part to the influence of the American-based fiddle star Michael Coleman, whose fluid, often florid playing appeared on countless 78rpm records in the 1920s and 30s, providing aspiring Irish fiddle players with a formidable level of virtuosity to emulate. It is a level easily matched by the likes of modern fiddlers such as Paddy, Seamus and Kevin Glackin, Mairead Ni Mhaonaigh and Maire Breatnach as well as others who have taken, and continue to take, their art to new heights.

The same is true of uillean pipers, most of whom play the modern instrument first developed by the Drogheda-born Taylor brothers in their Philadelphia workshop towards the end of the 19th century. Mellower in tone than their Scottish cousins, uillean pipes have enjoyed a surge in popularity during recent years, with the best

FINBAR FUREY

OPPOSITE The cognoscenti of fiddle music can tell where a player comes from by the style of playing.

ABOVE The outstanding Finbar Furey playing the uillean pipes, 1969.

BELOW Sharon Shannon, Ireland's foremost contemporary accordionist.

players able to conquer the instrument's complexity and produce music that is both evocatively haunting and brilliantly elaborate. The most outstanding modern exponents include Paddy Moloney, Finbar Furey, Davy Spillane and Maire Ni Ghrada, in whose hands the uillean pipes become worthy of awe and wonder.

It was not until the late 19th century that accordions and concertinas joined the arsenal of instruments employed by Irish musicians. For some unknown reason, the people of County Clare seized on the concertina with especial enthusiasm, and it was musicians from that region who achieved pre-eminence in Dublin when they came a'calling. Their arrival was not welcomed by all, however – a resistance most memorably summed up by the late musician/composer Sean O'Riada when he described accordions and concertinas as being 'designed by foreigners for the use of peasants with neither the time, inclination nor application for a worthier instrument'. Tell that to Sharon Shannon, unarguably Ireland's foremost contemporary accordionist, who makes a mockery of the American humorist Ambrose Bierce's description of her instrument as one '… in harmony with the sentiments of the assassin'.

The flute was taken up by Irish musicians – as it was by others across Europe – in the late 18th and early 19th centuries. Those unable to afford flutes (which obviously discounts the redoubtable classical flautist James Galway, owner of a solid gold

instrument) contented themselves with what were once dismissively called 'penny' whistles. To hear just what this humble instrument can do, one has only to listen to the recordings of Paddy Moloney of The Chieftains. His skill, ingenuity and imagination is typical of those who helped confirm the tin whistle an integral part of modern Irish music, while Matt Molloy (variously a member of The Bothy Band, Planxty and The Chieftains) has proved the same for the flute. The continued presence of these instruments – and the brilliance of their players – provide elements that are uniquely Irish.

BREAKING THROUGH THE BARRIERS

Down the years, Dublin obviously played host to the finest contemporary exponents of traditional music. It was the country's capital, after all, and you were not anyone until you had made it there. However, while there were (then as now) a myriad places in which the travelling soloist or group could dazzle the city's inhabitants and make a name for themselves, few 'traditional' musicians played outside Dublin's hostelries during the 200 or so years when Ireland was governed by Britain. Any unhappiness they may have felt at this ghetto-like scenario must have been mollified shortly after the purchase, in 1759, of Dublin's St James Gate Brewery by a gentleman called Arthur Guinness ...

Their music was deemed too Irish, too rumbustious and too unruly for the sensitive ears of the ruling and middle-classes who dominated Dublin society and viewed the country's working-class as little more than

OPPOSITE Classical Irish flautist James Galway – with his famous golden flute – performing at the BBC's *Proms in the Park*, 1996.

BELOW The Chieftains performing at Randalls Island Fleadh. The group successfully brought traditional Irish music to contemporary, mainstream audiences.

JAMES GALWAY

I know that my Redeemer liveth

G.F. Handel.

RIGHT Irish composer Michael William Balfe, who produced operas, operettas and many other classical works.

OPPOSITE Illustration dating from 1868 showing the music hall where the first-ever performance of Handel's *Messiah* took place in Dublin's Fishamble Street in 1742.

ignorant peasants who needed to be put – and kept – in their place, which was not, of course, at their grand balls, drawing-room soirées or concert evenings. Sadly, this bigotry was most pronounced among Anglo-Irish citizens apparently bent on proving themselves more Anglo than Irish.

There was the odd traditional musician who broke through those barriers of snobbery and outright racism, however. King George II was said to have been so impressed by the playing of a piper whom he heard during a visit to Dublin that he ordered a medal to be struck for him. There is every chance that the British monarch paid this tribute in 1742, for it was in that year that George was guest of honour at the first-ever performance of Handel's oratorio, *Messiah*. That took place at the long-gone concert hall in Fishamble Street, owned by Dublin's Charitable Music Society.

In truth, the only musicians, composers or singers genteel Dublin society would acknowledge or claim as their own during the 18th and 19th centuries were practitioners of classical music. There was, for example, the operatic tenor Michael Kelly, a son of Dublin who became one of Mozart's best friends and was rewarded with a starring role, in 1791, in the Vienna premiere of *The Magic Flute*. Sadly, the overwhelming success of that opera did nothing to halt Mozart's physical and financial decline, and he died shortly after. Michael Kelly's five minutes of fame were up.

In the 19th century, Dublin most notably produced the classical composer Michael William Balfe, although he – like Kelly – had to travel abroad to develop his career as a singer, conductor and writer. Leaving Ireland for London in 1823, when he was just 15 years old, Balfe studied in Italy under Rossini, and in 1833 returned to England to become conductor of the London Italian Opera. The composer of numerous operas, operettas and other works, Balfe is best remembered for *The Bohemian Girl*, an operetta that boasted the standard 'I Dreamed I Dwelt In Marble Halls', still a staple of song recitals the world over.

BEYOND THE PALE

In 1845 – two years after Balfe enjoyed a heady London season of champagne suppers on the back of *The Bohemian Girl* – word

traditional Irish music rather than signal its demise. For one, those who survived were quick to add to the song cannon with stories of hardship, the callous indifference of absentee landlords, or of triumph over disaster. More importantly, the emigrants took their music with them, its performance at weddings, wakes and baptisms (let alone when there was a bottle or two of some home-made brew to share) a vital link with former hearths, homes and loved ones.

Some Irish emigrants found themselves in the company of other Celts, most especially on Canada's eastern seaboard, where Bretons had settled as part of French colonization. The Highland clearances (those absentee English landlords again) had also exiled many Scots to the New World. As these subtly different Celtic traditions met, mixed and borrowed from each other, they were also enhanced by the folk tunes and styles of other European newcomers.

The establishment of Irish folk music as an American drawing-room staple was achieved in one stroke by the publication, in 1903, of *Music of Ireland*. The work of Francis O'Neill, a flute player from West Cork who had risen to become Chicago's general superintendent of police, what became known simply as 'The Book' not only put on record almost 2,000 traditional pieces that may have otherwise been lost, but offered them to a much wider audience who would, perhaps, have never otherwise encountered them.

Some of O'Neill's collected melodies were borrowed for popular songs, hymns and the hybrid folk music that transformed into what was pejoratively termed hillbilly music and became, in the 1920s and 30s, the beginnings of modern country music. These 'new' elements inevitably filtered back to Ireland, so it is no accident that Ireland has, for many years, enjoyed a lively country-music scene, and that Daniel O'Donnell – its most successful contemporary country star – enjoys a massive following in Britain, the US, Canada and Australia, all of which boast a large population of Irish extraction ready to support a winsome boy from 'back home'.

O'Donnell's success continues Ireland's other tradition of exporting pleasant, middle-of-the-road balladeers who became the predominant image of Ireland between the

reached Dublin that matters outside the Pale (the relatively small region of the capital in which British authority was both absolute and enforceable) had taken a substantial turn for the worse: the nation's potato fields were stricken with a devastating virus. During the next five years, more than a million Irish men, women and children died of starvation and disease, while a million or more fled the famine by emigrating to the United States, Canada and Australia. Paradoxically, this awful tragedy served to preserve and expand

DANIEL O'DONNELL

OPPOSITE An illustration from 1847 showing a woman and her children searching for potatoes during the potato famine of 1845. Paradoxically, this helped to preserve Irish music, as new songs about the hardships of the time were composed, and Irish people fleeing the famine spread Celtic music beyond Irish shores.

ABOVE Daniel O'Donnell, Ireland's foremost country-music exponent, enjoys worldwide success, particularly in those countries with a large Irish-related population.

VAL DOONICAN

1920s and 1960s. Thus, the likes of John McCormack, Josef Locke, Father Sydney MacEwan, Brendan O'Dowda, Bridie Gallagher, Dermot Henry, Delia Murphy and Val Doonican (among many others) also helped promote and sustain a cloying, saccharin-sweet confection of a rural idyll that owed less to reality than it did to the imagination of professional Tin Pan Alley songsmiths, who churned out many a paean of praise to a mist-wreathed Emerald Isle peopled by charming dimwits whose silver-haired mammies (with ever-smiling eyes) still used spinning wheels in rose-strewn cottages, ideally placed on the banks of the Shannon.

VENUES: SURVIVORS OF A GOLDEN ERA

Many of the Dublin music halls and theatres in which those artists once performed have now, sadly, vanished – making way, inevitably, for cinemas, bingo halls or yet more office blocks. Thus, the Rotunda Music Hall (once part of the Rotunda Gardens and site of an allegedly winning appearance by Brendan Behan in a talent competition as 'The Singing Blind Newsboy') lives only in memories. These days, its

BELOW Irish tenor Joseph Locke, whose story – he fled from public view to avoid tax evasion charges – was recounted in the movie *Hear My Song*.

ABOVE John McCormack, whose songs helped to sustain a saccharin-sweet stereotypical image of Ireland and its people.

OPPOSITE Irish crooner Val Doonican, singing in his trademark rocking chair.

FOLLOWING PAGE The Clancy Brothers (l to r: Liam Clancy, Tom Clancy, Paddy Clancy, Tommy Makem), who electrified American audiences with their performances of traditional Irish songs.

Round Room houses the Ambassador Cinema and the former Supper Room is home to the Gate Theatre.

The Crow Street Theatre has gone, too – it has been replaced by a musical instrument store. There is a supermarket just off O'Connell Street that was once the beautiful Scala Opera House. The Gaiety Theatre lives on, but will never again see the heady days when entertainer Maureen Patton filled the place for 12 weeks a year – six weeks around Christmas, and another six in the summer. Once the home of Irish opera, it was also the scene of Luciano Pavarotti's first Dublin appearance.

Another rare survivor of that golden era is the Olympia Theatre. Originally built as a music hall by the entertainer Dan Lowry, it is now one of Dublin's busiest rock venues in a city awash with places where live music is offered seven days a week, 52 weeks every year, including many dedicated to a new folk tradition that is very much alive and kicking.

If truth be told, that tradition was aided rather than hampered by Ireland's sufferance of two centuries of British rule, for nothing so encourages a movement – whether political or artistic – than its attempted suppression by outsiders. It also proved the inspiration for the renaissance of Celtic folk music that began in the US folk boom of the early 60s. Then it was led by the redoubtable Clancy Brothers (Liam, Paddy and Tom) and Tommy Makem. Exiles from Tipperary and Armagh respectively, their performances of traditional Irish songs electrified American audiences.

One of their most avid fans was the young Bob Dylan, and he 'borrowed' the melody of their anthemic 'The Patriot Game' to write 'With God On Our Side'. This epitomizes the continued mix-and-match process neatly, for the tune of 'The Patriot Game' owed its origins to an adaptation, by Dominic Behan, of an American pop song, 'Hear the Nightingale Sing', which had been recorded by Jo Stafford and Patti Page.

FOLK REVIVAL

The Dublin heart of this early 60s folk revival was O'Donoghue's, in Merrion Row. Still one of Ireland's leading music pubs, O'Donoghue's was the watering hole of choice for the likes of Joe Heaney, a gifted singer in the 'sean nos' (old-style) tradition,

OPPOSITE The Olympia Theatre, a former music hall, is now one of Dublin's busiest rock venues, with performances by a host of international stars, including Dublin's best.

BELOW Bob Dylan performing at Farm Aid. Dylan, a fan of The Clancy Brothers, used the melody of their song 'The Patriot Game' for his 'With God On Our Side'.

and uillean piper Seamus Ennis, both of whom passed on their genius to a younger generation of singers and musicians. Among those who graduated from O'Donoghue's were Ronnie Drew (who would go on to form The Dubliners folk group) and fiddler Sean Keane (later to become a member of The Chieftains).

This, of course, brings us neatly to the transformation of Irish Celtic music from back-room entertainment to international concert hall prominence. Appointed musical director of the Abbey Theatre in the early 1960s, Sean O'Riada invited Paddy Moloney to help create an authentic Irish 'soundtrack' for occasional dramatic productions. The team they formed, named Ceoltoiri Chualann, would inspire Moloney to form The Chieftains, a group who would never play in pubs or bars but who would bring traditional Irish music to a contemporary, mainstream audience.

Thirty-some years later, Moloney's lead has resulted not only in The Chieftains becoming one of the most popular and influential musical ensembles in the world, with more than 30 best-selling albums to their credit, recording in places as far apart as Nashville and China with guest singers as varied as Mick Jagger, Ry Cooder, Joni Mitchell, Tom Jones, Van Morrison, Chet Atkins, Willie Nelson, Sting and Sinead O'Connor, but also a cited inspiration for a vast number of young, second-generation, Irish folk-based stars far too numerous to mention here.

ABOVE LEFT Dublin's Abbey Theatre, c1930, where Sean O'Riada became musical director in the 1960s and helped to promote Irish music.

ABOVE RIGHT Performing over pints of Guinness in O'Donoghue's, one of Ireland's leading music pubs. The venue was at the heart of the revival of Irish folk music that took place in the 1960s.

BELOW The Dubliners folk group, formed by Ronnie Drew, who perfected his music in O'Donoghue's alongside many other famous 60s musicians.

Suffice it to say that there would be no Corrs, no Clannad, Altan, Enya or Riverdance without The Chieftains, and Ireland's new-found success around the world of popular music would have a very different slant if The Chieftains had never existed. There would be no U2, Thin Lizzy or Rory Gallagher, no Afro-Celtic sound system with its fascinating fusion of West African and Celtic 'roots' music, no Saw Doctors, no Cranberries, no Mary Black, Horslips, Planxty or Moving Hearts, and no Boomtown Rats.

BELOW The rock band U2, Ireland's most famous and successful musical export, hail from Dublin.

ABOVE Powerscourt
Townhouse Centre treats
visiting shoppers to free
lunchtime concerts.

OPPOSITE, ABOVE The
Corrs, one of Ireland's
most popular exports.

OPPOSITE, BELOW It is not
just rock bands like U2 of
which Dublin can boast:
Boyzone enjoys a massive
following, though mainly of
the young female variety.

The city of Dublin – now, more than ever – is the focal point of a nation in which one of the most vibrant traditional music forms in the world now rubs unselfconscious shoulders with all kinds of modern music, from rock and blues to free-form jazz.

The Temple Bar area – the very heartbeat of the city – thrums with energy, and live music is featured in scores of clubs and pubs in the district. International superstars now include Dublin on their tour schedules as a matter of course, for the city now boasts huge venues as disparate as The Point (three times host to the Eurovision Song Contest and scene of country star Garth Brooks' netting a remarkable $1,806,204 for the eight shows he staged there in 1994), and the sports stadia at Croker Park and Lansdowne Road, both of which have learned to live (and move) with the times.

Besides The Corrs, the world's pop charts can reasonably be said to have been conquered by the likes of Boyzone and B*witched. When the Celtic tiger roars, it seems that everyone listens.

All year round there are Celtic music festivals taking place somewhere in Ireland, from Derry to Cork, which now also boasts a prestigious annual international jazz festival every October. Kilkenny stages the Carlsberg Country Roots bonanza in May, and Killarney holds a country music festival each April. Dublin itself plays host to the annual Guinness Blues Festival in July, a month after the Liberties Festival sees the city immersed in a feast of music, parades, street theatre, art exhibitions and story-telling sessions.

Ireland, it is fair to say, has come a long way from the time when the only entertainment was to be had listening to some wee man beating on a bodhrán.

MYTHS

& LEGENDS
146–165

Dublin's Dun Laoghaire harbour is Ireland's foremost ferry port. Dublin owes its name to water: the original Dubh Linn means 'Black Pool', and the city's Irish name, Baile Átha Cliath, means 'Town of the Hurdle Ford', after the hurdles once erected there to prevent flooding.

Over a thousand years old, situated by the sea and dissected by the River Liffey, Dublin owes both its location and name to water. Its natural harbour and the confluence of the Liffey with the rivers Podder, Dodder and Tolka, which offered not only fresh water but also routes to the interior of the country, made this an obvious site for settlement.

EBLANA

ABOVE The harbour of Dun Laoghaire, in the suburbs of Dublin, is named after a fort that once existed there, believed to have been the residence of Laoghaire, a High King of Ireland converted to Christianity by St Patrick in the 5th century.

OPPOSITE Illustration depicting the death of the aged Irish king Brian Boru at the hands of Brodar the Viking. Brian became High King of Ireland in 1002 and was renowned for his beneficent rule.

THE ORIGINS OF DUBLIN

The Romans knew the settlement as Eblana, as shown in a Roman map dating from AD 140. The Irish name for Dublin – Baile Átha Cliath (pronounced Valya Aw Clia) – goes back to the time of the ancient Irish king Conor mac Nessa. When the Liffey flooded, Conor had a ford built from hurdles and boughs, and named the site the 'Town of the Hurdle Ford', or Baile Átha Cliath.

Water also features in the name 'Dublin'. In the 9th century, Vikings invaded and set up home at the monastic settlement of Dubh Linn – meaning 'Black Pool' in Irish – located on the site of the present gardens overlooked by Dublin Castle. Over time, Dubh Linn became Dublin.

In 1014, the Danes were finally defeated in the Battle of Clontarf, the 'Meadow of Bulls', which took place just north of Dublin. The day was Good Friday, chosen by the Danes as auspicious for them and inauspicious for the Christian Irish forces, led by the legendary Brian Boru, or Boroma. Brian had been king of Munster, but became High King of Ireland in 1002. Such was the beneficence of his rule that, as the bard McLaig sang in praise of the king, 'a young lady of great beauty, adorned with jewels and costly dress, might perform unmolested a journey on foot through the Island, carrying a straight wand, on top of which might be a ring of great value' – in other words, life, chastity and property were safe under his rule. Sadly, Brian did not live to enjoy his victory, for, at the age of 80, he was too old to join in the fray, and was killed while praying in his tent, crucifix in hand, by Brodar the Viking. Discovered by the king's men, Brodar was immediately and cruelly despatched.

The defeated Danes were gradually assimilated into the native population, and converted to Christianity. Christ Church Cathedral stands on the site of an earlier wooden church built in approximately 1038 for the evocatively named Sitric Silkenbeard, Norse king of Dublin.

Another foreigner with an evocative name, who also came by sea and who played a crucial role not only in the history of Dublin but of the whole of Ireland too, was Strongbow, Earl of Pembroke. Leading his force of Anglo-Normans, Strongbow breached the city's walled defences in 1169 to pave the way for an English presence on Irish soil that was to last for seven centuries, only ending – for Eire at least – with the signing of the Anglo-Irish Treaty in 1921 and the establishment of an independent Irish state. The well-known phrase 'beyond the pale', meaning unacceptable or intolerable, relates to English rule in Ireland, for the Pale was a 15th-century term used to describe those districts colonized by England in the 12th

ABOVE A silver penny bearing the profile of one of Ireland's early kings, Shitric III.

RIGHT Engraving of Theobald Wolfe Tone, dated 1827. Wolfe, a prominent member of the United Irishmens Society, was imprisoned after taking part in the 1798 rebellion. He killed himself while awaiting execution in Dublin prison.

MICHAEL COLLINS

ABOVE This postcard of Michael Collins, leader of Sinn Féin, was a popular memento after his death in 1922. Collins negotiated the peace treaty with Britain in December 1921 that established the Irish Free State.

century, namely, Dublin, Cork, Drogheda, Waterford and Wexford. By the 16th century, however, the Pale had contracted to no more than a 32km (20m) stretch around Dublin. Areas outside it were beyond English control and were therefore 'beyond the Pale'.

REMEMBERING HEROES

No visitor to Dublin can escape the presence of those legendary figures who fought and died for Irish freedom, and whose passion and patriotism were summed up by the poet W B Yeats with the words, 'A terrible beauty is born …' Their ghosts are everywhere in the city, in its place names and monuments – Theobald Wolfe Tone, the 18th-century Irish nationalist; Daniel O'Connell, founder of the Catholic Association; Charles Stewart Parnell, leader of the Irish Nationalist party; Michael Collins, leader of Sinn Féin; the poet Patrick Pearse, a leader of the 1916 Easter Upising. The rising itself was commemorated on its 50th anniversary in 1966 by the opening of

the Garden of Remembrance at the northern end of Parnell Square, dedicated to all those who gave their lives for Irish independence.

Echoes of more ancient legends may also be found in these monuments to Irish nationalism. Fenian Street, east of Trinity College, recalls the Fenians, the secret Irish-American republican brotherhood established in 1858 and named after the Fianna, the semi-mythical, heroic warrior band led by Finn McCool (Fionn mac Cumaill or mac Cumhal), whose exploits were immortalized in the collection of tales known as the Fenian Cycle, or Fianaigheacht, the lore of the Fiana. According to one tradition, Finn and his men, including his son Oisín, are – like Arthur of the Britons – not dead but only sleeping, in an enchanted cave somewhere, waiting for the moment when they will rise again to save their land from oppression.

North-west of Fenian Street and close to O'Connell Bridge is a monument to Daniel O'Connell, 'the Liberator', who secured Catholic emancipation for Ireland in 1829. Among the figures around the base is Erin, holding up the Act of Emancipation that granted rights to Roman Catholics that had previously been denied them by virtue of their religion. Erin represents the sovereignty of Ireland, just as Britannia does that of Britain – in myth, female figures are often seen as personifications of the land and are therefore, by the same token, chosen to symbolize the sovereignty of nations.

DIVINE INTERVENTION

According to legend, Erin, or Eriu, was originally the wife of one of the ancient gods of Ireland, the Tuatha Dé Danann, the 'People of the Goddess Danu'. Erin, and two of the other divine wives, Fotla and Banba, all begged that Ireland be named after them. Their wish was granted but in the end it was only Erin who was remembered in the name of the country we know as Eire. (Since goddesses have a predilection for splitting into three different personas, the threesome of Erin, Fotla and Banba may just have been different faces of the one Erin.)

Another allusion to ancient Irish myth may be found in Dublin's Garden of Remembrance in the large bronze statue of the Children of Lir, created by Oisín Kelly. The legend concerns the four children of the

ABOVE Statue of Daniel O'Connell, erected in 1882 near O'Connell Bridge. The allegorical figures around the base of the monument feature characters from Irish mythology.

OPPOSITE Lithograph of Daniel O'Connell published in Paris c1820. O'Connell secured the Act of Emancipation in 1829, which gave Roman Catholics rights previously denied them by the British Protestant elite.

sea god Lir – Fionuala, the 'Maid of the Fair Shoulder', her twin brother Aedh, 'Fire', and another pair of twins, the brothers Fiachra and Conn, who come to grief at the hands of their jealous stepmother, Aoife, who changes them into swans on Lake Darvra (Derryvaragh) in West Meath. Their enchantment is to last 900 years – three hundred on Lake Darvra; three hundred on the Straits of Moyle between Ireland and Scotland; and three hundred on the 'Western Sea' (the Atlantic) by Erris and Inis Glora – and will only end when the 'Man of the North' (Lairgnen, king of Connacht) marries the 'Woman of the South' (Deocha, princess of Munster). All that the children have left are their human voices and their song, and so magical is their singing that it dispels all sorrow and fills the hearer's soul with a deep sense of peace.

Towards the end of the 900 years, the children find themselves on Inis Glora, where, for the first time, they hear the ringing of a Christian bell from the chapel of St Kennock. The holy man instructs them in the faith, and fashions for them two silver neck-chains – one to join Fionuola to Aedh, the other Fiachra to Conn. By this time, Deocha has married Lairgnen and wants the wonderful singing swans as a wedding gift. When Lairgnan tries to take them from Kennock by force, pulling at their neck-chains, their feathers fall away to reveal not the beautiful beings they once were, but four old, bent and white-haired figures.

Knowing that their end is near, Fionuola begs Kennock to give them a Christian burial, there on Inis Glora, and to place their bodies in death as in life – Fionuola at the centre, Fiachra on her left, Conn on her right and Aedh before her face, for this was how she sheltered them on many a wild winter's night all alone on the sea. This Kennock does, and as he completes the sacred ceremony, he has a vision of four radiant faces and sees four shining swan-souls flying up to heaven.

A LAND OF HERO TALES, LOVE STORIES AND TRAGEDIES

Conor mac Nessa, the king who gave Dublin its Irish name Baile Átha Cliadh, also has mythological connections. Referred to alternatively as Conchobar, Conor was the king at whose court Cú Chulainn was

ABOVE Cú Chulainn (shown carrying the figure across the river) is the greatest of the Irish mythological heroes.

OPPOSITE This illustration, *Lugh's Enclosure,* shows the sun god holding court. According to legend, Lugh was the father of Cú Chulainn.

BELOW Statue of Cú Chulainn in Dublin's General Post Office.

CÚ CHULAINN

brought up. Cú Chulainn is probably the greatest of all Irish mythical heroes, and a statue of him stands in the General Post Office on O'Connell Street, added when the building was restored after a fire gutted it during the Easter Upising of 1916 (the restored façade also includes a figure of Hibernia, the Latin name for Ireland and a variant of the Irish 'Erin').

The collection of tales in which Cú Chulainn features is known as the Ulster Cycle, and they are too extensive to detail here. Born as Setanta, the hero was the son of Dechtire, sister of Conchobar, and the god Lugh, who changed himself into a mayfly that Dechtire inadvertently swallowed when drinking a glass of wine. The boy achieved his new name when, still no more than a slip of a lad, he killed the ferocious hound that guarded the home of Culann, a wealthy smith; from that day forward, he was known as Cú Chulainn, the 'Hound of Culann'. The most famous legend surrounding the hero is the Tain Bo Cuailgné, the 'Cattle Raid of Cooley'. Concerning a dispute between Queen Medb of Connacht and her husband Ailill over their possessions, Medb's desire to acquire the Brown Bull of Cooley belonging to Dáire of Ulster, and the war that ensues, the story shows Cú Chulainn at his most superhuman and impressive.

Conor/Conchobar's name also appears in one of the most tragic love stories in Irish mythology, surrounding Deirdre (Derdriu), Queen of Sorrows, and Naoise and his brothers, the Sons of Usnach. Deirdre is the most beautiful woman in all of Ireland, but at her birth the druid Cathbad prophesies that she will bring her country to grief and bloodshed. Despite this warning, Conchobar claims her as his own, and keeps her hidden away from the eyes of other men until she is old enough to marry. However, as the time for the wedding grows nearer, Deirdre meets someone much more to her liking – the handsome Naoise, with 'hair as black as the raven's wing, cheeks as red as blood, and skin as white as snow'. The two elope together, accompanied by Naoise's brothers, finally fleeing for safety to Scotland. By means of a treacherous ruse, Conchobar persuades them to return. Back on Irish soil, however, Naoise and his brothers are killed by Eoghan son of Durthacht, and Conchobar takes Deirdre as

How Sir Tristram demanded La Belle Isoude daughter of King Anguisshe of Ireland for his uncle King Mark: and how he set sail to carry Isoude into Cornwall

his wife. For a year she stays in his palace, but never smiles once. One day, Conchobar, irritated and vengeful, asks her what she detests most on earth. Her answer is clear – Conchobar himself and Eoghan – at which the king tells her that she will now have the pleasure of spending a year with her lover's murderer. As Eoghan is about to bear her off in his chariot, Deirdre jumps from it, shattering her head on a rock, and dies.

Another tale of tragic love is recalled in the village called Chapelizod, near the southwest corner of Phoenix Park on the western side of Dublin. Chapelizod is named after Isoud (also spelt Iseult and Isolde, among other variations) whose story, involving her lover Tristram, is one of the most famous of all medieval romances. Although it does not strictly form part of the body of Irish myth, the Irish connection lies in the fact that Iseult is an Irish princess, daughter of King Aengus. Tristram, for his part, is the nephew of King Mark of Cornwall, sent by Mark to bring 'Iseult the Fair' back to be Mark's bride. The plan goes wrong, however, when on the return voyage Tristram and Iseult inadvertently drink the love potion intended by Iseult's mother for her daughter and her husband-to-be. Despite their love, Iseult marries Mark, and Tristram eventually marries another Iseult – 'of the White Hands' – a princess of Britanny.

Towards the end of the tale, when Tristram lies wounded and near to death, he sends for Iseult the Fair, for he knows that she is the only one who can heal him. If she consents to come, the ship must sail white sails, he says; if she refuses, the sails must be black. Iseult does come, but when Tristram asks his wife what colour the sails are, she can think only of the greater love her husband has always felt for her rival. 'The sails are black,' she lies, at which Tristram turns his face to the wall and dies. When Iseult the Fair discovers Tristram dead, she dies, too. The pair are buried in one grave, on which a rose tree and a vine are planted, and – like the yew trees over the graves of Deirdre and Naoise – the two become so entwined that none can part them.

CHRISTIAN SAINTS

As well as these associations with mythological characters and with legendary figures in Irish history, Dublin also

remembers various Christian saints, around whom some fascinating tales have been woven. St Audoen's Church of Ireland on High Street, one of the oldest churches in Dublin, was originally built in 1190 and was dedicated to Ouen or Audoen, a 7th-century bishop of Rouen. Ouen was believed to have had extraordinary healing powers, in particular the ability to restore hearing to the deaf – a power that did not diminish even in death, for his relics still retained curative properties. In the porch of the St Audoen's Church is an ancient Christian gravestone known as the 'Lucky Stone', of which many strange tales are told.

On the site of St Audoen's there once stood an even more ancient Celtic church dedicated to one of the most revered of all Irish saints – St Columba or Columcille, the patron saint of poets. Born at Garton in Donegal, Columba took holy orders at Gasnevin. Among the monasteries he founded in Ireland is the monastery of Kells in County Meath, where the world-famous

ABOVE The oldest church in Dublin, named in honour of St Audoen.

BELOW Columba, patron saint of poets, was born in Ireland in AD 521.

DUBLIN

160

COLUMBA

Book of Kells, the 8th-century illuminated
manuscript of the Gospels, was produced
(it is now housed in Dublin's Trinity College);
he also founded the monastery on Iona, or
Holy Island, in the Hebrides, in 563. In 565,
Columba left for Scotland on his mission to
convert the pagan Picts. An accomplished
poet and scribe, he had a voice that reputedly
could be heard over a mile away, and his word
carried extraordinary force. One miracle
attributed to him tells how he killed a
dangerous wild boar with nothing more than
the power of his word; another recounts how
he banished a monster from Loch Ness with
the force of his prayers. The Cathach, a
psalter that he inscribed, was used in battle so
that those who held it would be under his

protective power. St Bride, another important figure in Celtic Christianity, is remembered in Bride Street, named after the now-demolished St Bride's Church with origins going back to pre-Viking times. Candlemas, her feast day on 1 February, was also known as Imbolc, the ancient Celtic festival of spring, and the saint's popularity is said to have been a continuation of the cult of her namesake, Brigit or Brígh, one of the most important Celtic goddesses. Goddess of wisdom and poetry, Brigit had two sisters of the same name who presided over leechcraft and smithwork.

Even more revered than either Bride or Columba is St Patrick (c390–c461), the patron saint of Ireland, whose cathedral stands in St Patrick's Close. Situated near the junction of six ancient routes known as Cross Poddle, a church has stood on this site – and been associated with Patrick – since the 5th century. It was St Patrick who was responsible for the spread of Christianity in Ireland. Many legends and miracles are attributed to him. He is said to have used the shamrock, with its leaf divided into three, to illustrate the oneness of the Holy Trinity; the shamrock, as a result, has become the national emblem of Ireland. He is also credited with banishing snakes from the island, and is therefore invoked by those afraid of snakes.

Near the cathedral, in St Patrick's Park, is a stone marking the site of St Patrick's Well, which, according to legend, the saint caused to spring from the earth. Until the Middle Ages, the well was believed to have miraculous healing properties.

On Francis Street, a much more modern church, built in 1830 to celebrate Catholic

OPPOSITE St Patrick, the patron saint of Ireland. Many churches and edifices in Ireland are dedicated to the saint, and his feast day is celebrated in Dublin with a parade on 17 March each year.

BELOW St Bride, who founded the first monastery in Ireland at Kildare. Her popularity is probably a continuation of the cult of her namesake, Brigit, the Celtic goddess of wisdom and poetry.

emancipation, is St Nicholas of Myra, dedicated to the saint better known as Santa Claus. Nicholas was a 4th-century bishop of Myra (now Mugla in south-west Turkey), and the stories surrounding him reveal a remarkable love and kindness. One tells how he saved three girls from prostitution by providing them with dowries so that they could marry, but the most famous tale recounts how he discovered three boys who had been murdered by a butcher and hidden in a tub, and brought them back to life. Tales of his generosity to children have merged with other folklore traditions to produce the modern Santa Claus.

Another saint associated with love – but not, in this case, of children – is St Valentine, the patron saint of lovers, whose remains lie in the Carmelite church on Whitefriar Street. The saint, who lived in the 3rd century, was executed in Rome, and his remains were brought from there in a steel casket in 1836. Various theories have been put forward to explain his connection with lovers. One is that his feast day falls on 14 February, the day when, according to folklore, birds choose their mates. The date of his feast day also coincides with the ancient Roman fertility festival of Lupercalia, held in mid-February. Whatever the truth of the matter, the saint has been invoked by lovers since medieval times and the St Valentine's tradition is now well established, ensuring continuing renown for the mysterious saint who now lies at rest in a Dublin church.

ABOVE Victorian Valentine card. St Valentine, who lived in the 3rd century, died in Rome but his remains were returned to his native Ireland in 1836, and now lie in the Carmelite church in Dublin.

RIGHT Illustration from a 16th-century Flemish *Book of Hours* depicting St Nicholas, famed for his love, kindness and generosity to children.

SANTA CLAUS

ABOVE Interior of Dublin's church of St Nicholas of Myra, dedicated to the 4th-century bishop who is now better known around the world as Santa Claus.

SPORT
166–187

Offaly fans at Croke Park cheering on their team at the All-Ireland hurling final, September 1998. This spectacular sport is the Irish national game, and its origins can be traced back to the Irish mythological hero Cú Chulainn, who, according to legend, won a match single-handedly against 150 opponents.

uíbh fhá

FIDEL

As the principal city of a supremely sports-minded nation, Dublin is host to many great set-piece sporting occasions. The annual All-Ireland hurling and football finals at Croke Park; Rugby Union internationals at Lansdowne Road; the Classic race meetings, and the Dublin Horse Show; the climax of the Ras Tailtainn cycle race; and major golf championships are highlights of a full sporting calendar. Both visitors and natives flock to these events with the added knowledge that Dubliners — being people who think highly of fun — combine their sporting tastes with the Irish knack of easy hospitality, and invest the proceedings with an element of carnival.

OPPOSITE The 1995
Dublin Horse Show at
Ballsbridge. The horse
show, which takes place
each August, is a premiere
social event as well as a
sporting one.

ABOVE The Artane Boys
Band playing in Croke Park.
Dublin is renowned for its
good-humoured approach
to sporting events, which
frequently have a carnival-
like atmosphere.

BELOW Competitors at the
Tailtainn Games of 1922,
which took place in Croke
Park to celebrate Irish
sport and culture.

THE POLITICS OF SPORT

Parallel with Dubliners' love of sporting fun
has been Dublin's experience that, in Ireland,
nothing lacks a political dimension. The city
has seen the often-conflicting cultural and
political traditions of Ireland reflected on
sporting fields of play. In Dublin, the
sporting manifestations of the island's
diversity have frequently met, clashed and
sometimes been reconciled.

The most dramatic instance of this facet of
Dublin's sporting life took place on the
original Bloody Sunday. During the morning
of 21 November 1920, on the orders of
Michael Collins, 12 British officers and
agents were assassinated.

That afternoon, a Gaelic football match
between Dublin and Tipperary took place at
Croke Park, in north Dublin on the banks of
the Royal Canal; the proceeds, it was said,
were intended to buy arms for the Irish
Volunteers. With just a quarter of an hour to
play, a combined body of Black & Tans and
Dublin Metropolitan Police entered the
stadium and commenced firing
indiscriminately. Between 12 and 14 people
were killed, including Tipperary back
Michael Hogan, for whom the present Hogan
stand is named.

Croke Park is named for Thomas William
Croke, Archbishop of Cashel, a strong
supporter of the early efforts to revive
Ireland's traditional games. The ground dates
from the mid-19th century, when it was
known as Jones Road Sport & Recreation
Ground, and, alternatively, as the City &
Suburban Racecourse. It was purchased in

ABOVE The All-Ireland hurling final in September 1991, featuring Tipperary vs Kilkenny. Although Dublin does not have a strong reputation in the sport of hurling, matches still attract plenty of fans.

1908 by Frank Dineen, a member of the Gaelic Athletic Association, from whom the GAA itself acquired it in 1913.

HURLING

The Gaelic Athletic Association was founded in 1884, its primary expressed aim being 'to bring hurling back to Ireland'. Perhaps the most spectacular of all team sports, hurling is the Irish national game, with roots in pre-Christian history. Irish annals record that in 1272 BC a hurling match developed into a full-scale military engagement, known as the Battle of Moytura. The game recurs throughout Irish legend, the most notable instance being the tale of the great hero Cú Chullain playing and winning a match single-handedly against 150 opponents.

The founders of the GAA – notably Michael Cusack and Maurice Davin – fully intended the association to be part of the general national revival, characterized politically in the Home Rule and Land League agitation, and culturally with the establishment in 1893 of the Gaelic League. In this they enjoyed the support of the Irish parliamentary leader, Charles Stewart Parnell.

The fathers of the GAA were also acting in conscious reaction to the increasingly sophisticated organization and popularity of what they regarded as the 'foreign' games of rugby, cricket and association football. This attitude led to the famous GAA ban, by which all members were forbidden to play, organize or even watch any but the 'national' games of hurling, Gaelic football, camogie (women's hurling), handball and Irish rounders (a game similar to softball, and also utilizing the sliothar – the ball used in hurling). The ban was abolished in 1971, but

RIGHT Hurling bears a resemblance to hockey, but in hurling, the ball can be carried along on the flat end of the sticks and even hit in the air.

CROKE PARK

ABOVE Fans walking the streets of Dublin on Gaelic cup final day 1997.

OPPOSITE Dalymount Park, home to the Bohemian Football Club, was founded in 1890. The park is Ireland's national stadium for association football.

FOLLOWING PAGE Ireland vs Wales playing in 1994 at Lansdowne Road rugby ground. Visitors who come to watch the Five Nations matches that are held here always enjoy the wonderful atmosphere of Dublin's rugby mecca.

it had always been less zealously observed in Dublin than in rural areas of Ireland. Even the most patriotic of Dubliners were known to desert Croke Park occasionally, and head up the North Circular Road to watch the Bohemians soccer club play in Dalymount Park – Ireland's national stadium for association football. Another instance of Dubliners showing themselves unwilling to be dictated to in sporting matters occurred in 1955. With the Republic of Ireland scheduled to play a friendly match against Yugoslavia at Dalymount Park – the first visit to Ireland by an Iron Curtain country – John Charles McQuaid, the notoriously authoritarian archbishop of Dublin, used the city's pulpits in urging all good Catholics to boycott the match against these representatives of 'Godless Communism'. In the event, the match was a sell-out, and the overflowing queues wanting tickets included many staunch GAA supporters.

In the GAA games, Dublin has traditionally never been much of a power in hurling, although the county has had periods of success at Gaelic football. During the 1970s and early 80s, the 'Dubs' competed in several All-Ireland championships – notably the sequence of epic finals against Kerry in 1975, 76, 78 and 79 – and gained a strong local following.

James Joyce, in the Cyclops chapter of *Ulysses*, used Michael Cusack as a model for the character of The Citizen – the embodiment, as Joyce saw it, of narrow, xenophobic, literally one-eyed nationalism. When entering a public house, Cusack habitually greeted barmen with the words 'I'm citizen Cusack from the parish of Carron in the barony of Burran in the county of Clare, you Protestant dog!' It is ironic, then, that Cusack had been a highly skilled player as a young man, and later coach of the 'foreign' game of Rugby Union football.

RUGBY

Irish rugby enthusiasts enjoy perpetuating the notion that William Webb Ellis – the Rugby schoolboy who first picked up the ball and ran with it – was actually born in Ireland, but evidence for this is tenuous. The game in Ireland was developed, in the main, by students at Trinity College in Dublin. TCD Rugby Club was formed in 1854, and is the

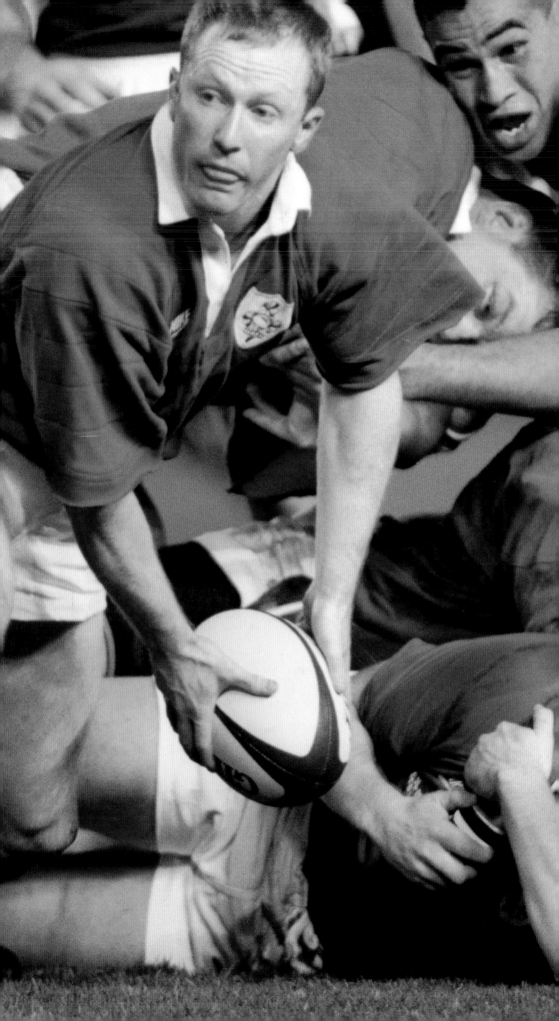

second oldest in the world. Various club combinations continued during the 1860s and early 1870s, while parallel developments took place in the north of Ireland. In December 1874, at a meeting held in John Lawrence's sporting goods shop in Grafton Street, a combined Irish Rugby Football Union was formed. The first international to be played in Dublin took place almost exactly one year later. The match, played at Leinster cricket ground, Rathmines, saw England beat Ireland by a score of 8–0.

Edmund Van Esbeck, in his centenary history of the IRFU, remarks that '… Lansdowne Road holds a special place in the hearts of all rugby men'. The ground, leased from the Pembroke Estate, was first developed by William Henry Dunlop as a modest multi-purposed stadium seating 400, and featuring a cinder track, cricket pitch and football ground. In 1908, a new lease was negotiated with Lord Pembroke and ambitious improvements were undertaken. Further modifications were made in 1928 and 1955, and the modern stadium, straddling the south Dublin suburban railway lines, was finally completed in 1977.

Rugby in Dublin – as in most of Ireland with the exception of Limerick City – has tended to be a middle-class sport, traditionally played mainly in the Protestant academies, or by the more exclusive Catholic schools such as Belvedere College. In the past, Ireland has enjoyed considerable success at international level, despite having a relatively

OPPOSITE Ireland's Niall Hogan photographed delivering the ball from a ruck during the Ireland vs Western Samoa match at Lansdowne Road, 1996.

BELOW England's Lawrence Dallaglio being successfully tackled by Ireland's Kevin Maggs during the 1999 Five Nations match at Lansdowne Road. In the end, though, Ireland lost by 15 to 27.

ABOVE George Best, one of the greatest footballers of all time, going onto the pitch for Manchester United in 1972. He is just one of Ireland's many great sporting exports.

ABOVE Irishman Liam Brady of Arsenal during a Liverpool vs Arsenal charity shield in August 1979.

small pool of players to draw upon. The recent professionalism of Rugby Union has made the future more problematic. In any case, Dubliners of all classes relish the Five Nations Championship matches, and create an atmosphere at Lansdowne Road that visiting fans always find memorable. The ground also remains home to the Lansdowne and Wanderers Rugby Clubs, and since 1971 has diversified to become a venue for other games, notably soccer.

SOCCER

Association football in Ireland has had a chequered history. Caught between the rock of rugby and the hard place of the GAA ban, the game has often struggled for both players and support. Since 1921, soccer in Ireland has had two (often antagonistic) governing bodies: the Irish Football Association, based in Belfast, and the Football Association of Ireland, based in Dublin. There has been much chopping, changing and reorganizing of clubs. Continuing Dublin teams have included Shamrock Rovers, the most consistently successful of Irish clubs, the Bohemians and Shelbourne, whose stadium is at Ringsend.

League football in Ireland is, in the main, semi-professional, and the quality of play has suffered through a continuing exodus of the best players to clubs in Britain. Many Irish players – including Dubliners like Liam Brady and David O'Leary – have become stars in English football. Over the years, some have lamented that soccer, unlike rugby, lacked a 32-county Irish national team. In 1971, Irish football fans had a glimpse of what such a team might accomplish. In the first game to be played under the Association

RIGHT Association football player David O'Leary representing his home country, Eire.

Code at Lansdowne Road in modern times, a charity friendly took place between Brazil (with Pele in the side), and an All-Ireland team, which included such Northern Ireland luminaries as George Best as well as stars from the Republic. In an exhilarating and highly entertaining match, Brazil overcame a 3–1 Irish lead to win 4–3.

The dreams aroused by such occasions were buoyed in 1986 when the FAI – showing a refreshing lack of parochial nationalism – engaged Jack Charlton, a star of England's 1966 World Cup winners, as national team manager. Charlton introduced a style of play that did not please every purist – and tracing the Irish connections of some of his players was a challenge to genealogists – but he did bring unprecedented success to the Republic of Ireland team. The country qualified for the European championships in 1988, and for the World Cup Finals in both 1990 and 1994. In the process, Charlton became a national hero, and football hysteria swept the population. A notable feature of this Dublin

ABOVE The 1994 World Cup Mexico vs Republic of Ireland match. Although Mexico won 2–1, Irish jubilation at reaching the World Cup finals, under the management of Jack Charlton, was immense.

LEFT Jack Charlton became manager of the Republic of Ireland soccer team in 1986. Although an Englishman, Charlton is now an Irish national hero, having twice taken the country to the World Cup finals, in 1990 and 1994.

football mania was the continuing ability of Irish supporters to make an almost invariably good-natured party of their sporting occasions. The Dublin fans' reputation for amiability makes the forced abandonment of a recent match at Lansdowne Road due to violent and pre-meditated outrages by British neo-fascists even more shocking.

CRICKET

Of the other popular team games, cricket in Ireland is among the poorest of poor relations. The first recorded match in Dublin took place at Phoenix Park in 1792, between Colonel Lennox's English Garrison XI and a team designated as All-Ireland. The stake was 1000 guineas, and Colonel Lennox's side scooped it up. Cricket in Ireland is almost exclusively an urban pursuit. While both the quality of play and support are modest, one of Dublin's sporting pleasures is a balmy summer afternoon spent watching cricket in

Trinity's salubrious College Park. It might be argued that Dublin's most famous cricketer was the Trinity alumnus, Samuel Beckett. He played for the university, though admittedly, he seems to have been awarded his Nobel Prize for other accomplishments.

CHILDREN'S GAMES AND PUBLIC PARKS

In common with most modern cities, Dublin has seen a steady decline in children's street games and sports. Massive increases in traffic and the advent of television and video games have been accompanied by the withering away of what was once a vigorous inner-city culture of street football, and ball-bouncing and rope-skipping games, many played with rhyming and rhythmic accompaniment. What were once 'The Singing Streets' do not sing much anymore. Dublin also, with one exception, is not well-endowed with playgrounds. When the Wilde Streets Commission of the 18th and early 19th centuries laid out Dublin's Georgian squares and terraces, they included many commodious open spaces such as St Stephen's Green, and Mountjoy, Merrion and Fitzwilliam Squares. However, these were designed to be places of placid resort and sedate relaxation rather than playing fields, and they were certainly not intended for the promiscuous rough-and-tumble games of young 'chiselers' from the slums of Ballybough and the Liberties.

In compensation, Dublin boasts the Phoenix Park. Covering over 688 hectares (1700 acres) – more than twice the size of New York's Central Park – and with a circumference of 11km (7 miles), Phoenix Park is the largest enclosed park in Europe and one of the largest in the world. The lands, originally belonging to the Kilmainham Priory of St John, were confiscated during the 16th century and turned into a deer park. In 1671, Lord Ormonde landscaped the area, and the park was opened to the public by Lord Chesterfield in 1747. The name Phoenix Park is thought to be a corruption of the Irish *fionn uisca*: 'pure water'. The park has lakes and miles of paths winding through pleasant and varied horticultural displays, including the People's Garden at the southeast corner. The Zoological Gardens opened in 1830, making it the world's second oldest public

TOP Cyclists riding through Phoenix Park, one of the finest city parks in Europe.

ABOVE Wearing snakeskin at Phoenix Park Zoo, the second oldest in the world.

OPPOSITE Children jumping rope in York Street, Dublin. Sadly, this once-common sight of children playing games in the street is now as rare in Dublin as it is elsewhere.

zoo. The largest single section of Phoenix Park is the area known as the Fifteen Acres. Despite its name, this portion of the park, which is entirely devoted to playing fields, actually covers some 81 hectares (200 acres).

ATHLETICS AND BOXING

Apart from team games, other sporting activities popular with Dubliners include boxing and athletics. The Irish have a tradition of producing strong middle- and long-distance runners, typified by Ron Delany – winner of the 1500 metres Gold Medal at the 1956 Olympic Games in Melbourne – and Noel Carroll, who later became a government minister. The focal point for athletics in Dublin has been Santry Stadium in the north of the city.

From the Regency days of Pierce Egan – the Irish-born author of *Boxiana* – pugilism has always been popular with Irish people at home and overseas. As with her footballers, other athletes and the population in general, Ireland has exported a great deal of boxing talent. In the bare-knuckle era, Irish-American heavyweight champion John L Sullivan fought in Dublin. His successor, James J Corbett, did not box in Dublin, but in 1909 he did bring his music hall turn to the city. The shortest heavyweight championship bout on record took place in Dublin's Theatre Royal in 1908, when Tommy Burns knocked out Jem Roche in 88

STEVE COLLINS

STEVE COLLINS

BELOW Steve Collins vs Nigel Benn at the Nynex Arena in 1996. World Champion middleweight Collins, who stopped Benn at the end of round 6, is Dublin's greatest boxing hero in recent years. He retired in 1999.

seconds. In 1972, Mohammad Ali fought and won a bout in Dublin against Al 'Blue' Lewis. Dublin's boxing mecca is the National Stadium in the South Circular Road, a venue also for many music events. Dublin's greatest boxing hero in recent years has been Steve Collins, a native of the city, and World Champion middleweight until his retirement on medical advice in 1999.

DOG AND HORSERACING

Not far from the National Stadium, at Harold's Cross, is one of Dublin's two principal greyhound tracks, the other being at Shelbourne Park, near the Ringsend home of Shelbourne Football Club. Ireland has a long tradition of breeding and exporting dogs and horses for racing; the origins of both dog- and horse-breeding lie in the essentially rural activity of hunting. A highlight of the year for Irish horse-lovers, and a magnet for equine-minded visitors from all over the world, is the Dublin Horse Show, which takes place each August at the Royal Dublin Society Showgrounds in Ballsbridge. The RDS dates from 1731, and the horse show was initiated in 1868, and remains a premiere social event as well as sporting occasion.

Even with the recent demise of the Phoenix Park racecourse – which was physically nearest the city centre – there are still a number of courses adjacent to the city. These include Leopardstown, Punchestown, Baldoyle, Naas and the Curragh. Situated on the plains of Kildare, the Curragh – which in Irish means 'course for horses' – has seen horseracing since AD 250, being the scene of the annual fair of Aenach Colmain, at which horseraces played an important part. In modern times, the Curragh has become the administrative headquarters of both flat and National Hunt racing in Ireland, and is the venue for the Irish Derby and other Classic races.

It might be said that Dublin's racing fans – while enthusiastic punters – are rather removed from the sport's pastoral roots, and, unlike their country cousins, do not harbour much in the way of actual affection for the animals themselves. The playwright and author Brendan Behan – a quintessential north-side Dubliner – once observed that he was 16 years old before he discovered that horseracing was not all done with telephones.

SPORT

187

DUBLIN

TOP Illustration showing the opening of the new race stand on the Curragh of Kildare in 1853. Horseracing has taken place here since AD 250.

ABOVE Dublin has two main greyhound racing tracks: Harold's Cross and Shelbourne Park.

OPPOSITE Competitors at the 1991 Dublin Horse Show. Dublin's racing fans are enthusiastic punters, though perhaps not true horse lovers

DIRECTORY

ARCHITECTURE

Casino, Marino
off the Malahide Road
North Dublin
8331618

Christ Church Cathedral
Christchurch Place
visitors daily 10am–5pm

Custom House
Custom House Quay

The Clarence Hotel
6–8 Wellington Quay
Dublin 2
6709000

Dublin Castle
Castle Street

The Four Courts
Church Street

Kilmainham Gaol
Inchicore Road

Marsh's Library
St Patrick's Close

Newbridge House
Donabate
Co. Dublin
8436534

Rathfarnham Castle
Rathfarnham
Dublin 14
4939462

St Patrick's Cathedral
Patrick Street
visitors Monday to Friday,
9am–6pm

Trinity College
Dublin
6082242

ART

Apollo Gallery
18 Duke Street
Dublin 2
6725298

**Arthouse Multimedia Centre
for the Arts**
Curved Street
Temple Bar
Dublin 2
6056800

Combridge Fine Arts
17 South William Street
Dublin 2
6774652

Douglas Hyde Gallery
Trinity College
Dublin
6081116

The Frederick Gallery
24 South Frederick Street
Dublin 2
6707055

Gallery of Photography
Meeting House Square
Temple Bar
Dublin 2
6714654

Hallward Gallery
65 Merrion Square
Dublin 2
6621482

**Hugh Lane Municipal
Gallery of Modern Art**
Charlemont House
Parnell Square North
Dublin 1
8741903

**The Irish Museum of
Modern Art**
Royal Hospital
Military Road
Kilmainham
Dublin 8
00 3531 6129900

National Gallery of Ireland
Merrion Square West
Dublin 2
6615133

Oriel Gallery
17 Clare Street
Dublin 2
6763410

Solomon Gallery
Powerscourt Townhouse
Centre
South William Street
Dublin 2
6794237

Taylor Galleries
16 Kildare Street
Dublin 2
6766055

**Temple Bar Gallery and
Studios**
5–7 Temple Bar
Dublin 2
6710073

DRAMA & LITERATURE

Abbey Theatre
Lower Abbey Street
Dublin
8787222

Focus Theatre
6 Pembroke Place
Dublin 2
6763071

Gaiety Theatre
South King Street
6771717

Lambert Puppet Theatre
Clifton Lane
Monkstown
Co. Dublin
2800974

Players Theatre
Front Square
Trinity College
Dublin
6082242

Dublin Writers Museum
18 Parnell Square
Dublin 1
8722077

Shaw Birthplace
33 Synge Street
Dublin 8
4750854

Jameson Literary Pub Crawl
Starting from The Duke Pub
on Duke Street
4540228
Dublin 2

The James Joyce Centre
35 North Great Georges Street
Dublin 1
8788547

Oscar Wilde's Home
Number 1
North west corner of
Merrion Square
Dublin 2

FESTIVALS & RELIGION

Bloomsday
Week long festival in June
From Sandy Cove to other
Joyce related venues

Church of St Werburgh
Werburgh St
Dublin 8

Dublin International Film Festival
February/March
Irish Film Centre and other
venues

Dublin Theatre Festival
October
Various venues all over
Dublin

Feis Ceoil
March
Classical Music Festival
Various venues all over
Dublin

Historic Graves Tour
National Graves Association
8231312

Irish Jewish Museum
4 Walworth Road
Portobello
Dublin 8
4531797

1916 Rebellion Walking Tour
Guided walk through the
streets which played a part in
the Easter Rising

International Bar
Wicklow Street
6762493

St Mary's Pro–Cathedral
Cathedral Street
daily 8am–7pm

St Michan's Church
Church Street

St Patrick's Cathedral Choristors
Six days a week July/August

St Patrick's Day Festival
Four-day festival St Patrick's
Day Parade on 17 March
from St Stephen's Green to
Parnell Square

Temple Bar Fleadh
Three-day festival in March
Temple Bar

FOOD & DRINK

Delicatessens
The Big Cheese Company
St Andrew's Lane
Dublin 2
6711399

Magill's
14 Clarendon Street
Dublin 2
6713830

Pubs
The Brazen Head
20 Lower Bridge Street
Dublin 8
6795186

Davy Byrne's
21 Duke Street
Dublin 2
6779364

The Duke
Duke Street
Dublin 2
6799553

Horseshoe Bar
Shelbourne Hotel
St Stephen's Green
Dublin 2
67664716

Mulligans
8 Poolbeg Street
Dublin 2
6775582

The Stag's Head
1 Dame Court
Dublin 2
6793701

RESTAURANTS
Bad Ass Cafe
9 Crown Alley
Dublin 2
6712596

Blazing Salads
21c Powerscourt Townhouse
Centre
South William Street
Dublin 2
6719552

Chandni
174 Pembroke Road
Dublin 4
6681458

Eden
Meeting House Square
Temple Bar
Dublin 2
6764679

King Sitric
Harbour Road
Howth
Co. Dublin
8325235

Le Coq Hardi
35 Pembroke Road
Dublin 4
6689070

Mao
2 Chatham Row
Dublin 2
6704899

Mermaid Cafe
69 Dame Street
Dublin 2
6708236

NIco's
53 Dame Street
Dublin 2
6773062

Peacock Alley
Fitzwilliam Hotel
St Stephen's Green
Dublin 2
4787000

Pizza Stop
6 Chatham Lane
Dublin 2
6796712

Wongs
436 Clontarf Road
Dublin 3
8334400

Yamamori Noodles
71 South Great Georges
Street
Dublin 2
4755001

MUSIC

National Concert Hall
Earlsfort Terrace
Dublin 2
4751666

Bank of Ireland Arts Centre
Forster Place
Dublin 2
6711488

ROCK MUSIC
Break for the Border
Grafton Street Plaza Hotel
Johnsons Place
Dublin 2
4780300

Fibber McGees
80 Parnell Street
Dublin 1
8722575

Olympia
72 Dame Street
Dublin 2
6777744

The Point
East Link Bridge
North Wall Quay
Dublin 1
8363633

TRADITIONAL MUSIC

Harcourt Hotel
60 Harcourt Street
Dublin 2
4783677

Kitty O'Sheas
23 Upper Grand Sreet
Canal Street
Dublin 4
6609965

Mulligans
18 Stoneybatter
Dublin 7
6779249

Slatterys
Capel Street
Dublin 1
8727971

JAZZ

Hotel Pierre
Dun Laoghaire
2800291

Renards Jazz and Supper Club
33 South Frederick Street
Dublin 2
6775876

Sach's Hotel
21 Morehampton Road
Dublin 2
6680995

CLUBS

Annabel's
Burlington Hotel
Upper Leeson Street
Dublin 4
6605222

Club M
Blooms Hotel
6 Angelsea Street
Dublin 2
6715622

La Cave
28 South Anne Street
Dublin 2
6794409

The Kitchen
East Essex Street
Dublin 2
6776635

SPORT

Colours Boat Race
April
River Liffey

Dublin Horse Show
August
Royal Dublin Society
Showgrounds
Ballsbridge

Federation of Irish Cyclists
619 North Circular Road
Dublin 1
8551522

House of Sport
Long Mile Road
Walkinstown
Dublin 12
4501633

Gaelic Football
Cumann Luthchleas Gael
Croke Park
Dublin 3
8363222

Golfing Union of Ireland
Glencar House
81 Eglinton Road
Donnybrook
Dublin 4
2696244

International Rugby Championship
January/February
Matches at Landsdowne Road
Dublin

Irish Ladies Golf Union
1 Clonskeagh Square
Clonskeagh
Dublin 14
2696244

Irish Rugby Football Union
62 Landsdowne Road
Ballsbridge
Dublin 4
6684601

The Liffey Swim
September
From Watling Street Bridge to Custom House

Maracycle
June
Cycle marathon between Dublin and Belfast

National Sailing School
Dun Laoghaire
2844195

Soccer Football Association of Ireland
80 Merrion Square
Dublin 2
6766864

Tennis Ireland
Argyle Square
off Morehampton Road
Donnybrook
Dublin 4
6681841

PICTURE CREDITS

The publishers wish to thank the following individuals and organizations for their kind permission to reproduce the photographs in this book. Every effort has been made to credit the artists, photographers and organizations whose work has been included and the publishers apologise for any unintentional omissions.

James Adam & Sons 34 **AKG, London** front cover top, 58, 132 /Henning Bock 116 /Hugh Lane Municipal Gallery of Modern Art 73 bottom /Musei Civici, Padua 82 /National Museum of Ireland 35 bottom /Michael Teller front cover centre right, 8–9, 60, 95 bottom, 153 **Allsport** 83, 177, 185 /Simon Bruty 170 top, 170 bottom /Hulton Getty 178 /Inpho 179 bottom /Duncan Raban 179 top /Ben Radford 180 top Arcaid /Natalie Tepper 12 top **Arthouse** 44, 45 **Bridgeman Art Library, London/New York**/Bradford Art Galleries and Museums 158 /Fitzwilliam Museum, University of Cambridge 164 bottom /Philip Mould, Historical Portraits Ltd 59 /National Museum of Ireland 35 top /private collections 62, 97, 164 top /Julian Simon Fine Art Ltd 125 top /Yale Center for British Art, Paul Mellon Collection, USA 36 **Collections**/Ashley Cooper 13 /Michael Diggin 23 bottom /Geoff Howard 142 top right /Image Ireland 19, 112 bottom /Image Ireland /Thomas Ennis 10 /Image Ireland/Alain Le Garsmeur 53 /Image Ireland/Geray Sweeney 23 top, 25 top, 114 top /Julian Nieman 32–33, 52 top, 115 bottom, 118–119 /Mark O'Sullivan 68 bottom, 85 top /Brian Shuel 90 top, 94, 173 /Michael St Maur Shuel 30 top, 89, 90 bottom, 121, 168 /Geray Sweeney 26 top, 52 bottom, 85 bottom, 86, 95 top, 96, 101 bottom, 120 top, 120 bottom /George Wright 100 **Corbis UK Ltd**/Dave Bartruff 16–17 /Bettmann 163 /Michael Brennan 184 bottom /Richard Cummins 165 /Macduff Everton front cover inset /Catherine Karnow front cover centre left /Richard T. Nowitz 144 /Michael St Maur Shuel 181, 183 top /Ted Spieg 11 top /Jim Sugar 183 bottom /Tim Thompson 186 /Inge Yspeert 125 bottom **Michael Diggin** 6, 18 top, 28–29 **Mary Evans Picture Library** 61 top, 66, 72, 84, 157, 159, 160 bottom, 161, 162, 187 top **Werner Forman Archive**/National Museum of Ireland 11 bottom **Gallery of Photography**/Ross Kavanagh 42, 43 left, 43 right **Green on Red Gallery, Dublin** 41 **Hulton Getty Picture Collection** 37, 56–57, 63 top, 63 bottom, 64 left, 68 top, 70 left, 70 right, 71, 74, 75, 79, 80–81, 133, 134, 137 top, 142 top left, 146–147, 148, 149, 150 bottom, 151, 152, 169 bottom **Inpho** 172, 187 bottom /Patrick Bolger 166–167, 184 /Damien James 169 top /Lorraine O'Sullivan 87, 171, 174–175 /Billy Stickland 176, 180 bottom **Irish Museum of Modern Art** 48–49, 50 **Jaki Irvine/Douglas Hyde Gallery** 46, 47 **Kobal Collection** 65, 73 top /Beacon Communications /20th Century Fox 76–77 /Columbia 78 /Icon/Pathé 67 right /Warner Bros 69 **Octopus Publishing Group Ltd** 98–99, 101 top, 102, 104, 150 top, 156 top, 156 bottom, 182/Trinity College Library, Dublin back cover right **Redferns** front cover bottom /Brigitte Engl 128 /Patrick Ford 124, 129 bottom, 145 top /Glen Miles 122–123 /Leon Morris 127 /David Redfern 126, 131, 136, 137 bottom, 138–139 /Ebet Roberts 130, 141 /Brian Shuel 129 top, 142 bottom /Nicky J. Sims 145 bottom /Barbara Steinwehe 143 /Jon Super 135 **Neil Setchfield** 2, 5, 12 bottom, 14, 15, 18 bottom, 20, 21, 22 top, 22 bottom, 24, 25 bottom, 26 bottom, 27, 29, 30 bottom, 31, 40, 51, 54, 55, 61 bottom, 64 right, 67 left, 88, 91, 92–93, 103, 105, 106, 107, 108, 109, 110, 111, 112 top, 113, 114 bottom, 115 top, 117, 140, 154 top, 154 bottom, 155, 160 top **Tony Stone Images**/Joe Cornish back cover left **Taylor Galleries** 38–39